WELCOMING THE SAVING REIGN OF GOD

A Study of Isaiah

Jack W. Hayford
with
Joseph Snider

THOMAS NELSON PUBLISHERS
Nashville • Atlanta • London • Vancouver

Welcoming the Saving Reign of God
A Study of Isaiah
Copyright © 1996 by Jack W. Hayford

Published in Nashville, Tennessee, by Thomas Nelson, Inc.

Unless otherwise indicated, Scripture quotations are from the
New King James Version of the Bible, © 1979, 1980, 1982,
Thomas Nelson, Inc., Publishers

Printed in the United States of America
1 2 3 4 5 6 7 8 — 01 00 99 98 97 96

CONTENTS

· ·

Welcoming the Saving Reign of God (A Study of Isaiah) is one of a series of study guides that focus exciting, discovery-geared coverage of Bible book and power themes—all prompting toward dynamic, Holy Spirit-filled living.

About the Executive Editor

JACK W. HAYFORD, noted pastor, teacher, writer, and composer, is the Executive Editor of the complete series, working with the publisher in the conceiving and developing of each of the books.

Dr. Hayford is Senior Pastor of The Church On The Way, the First Foursquare Church of Van Nuys, California. He and his wife, Anna, have four married children, all of whom are active in either pastoral ministry or vital church life. As General Editor of the *Spirit-Filled Life® Bible*, Pastor Hayford led a four-year project, which has resulted in the availability of one of today's most practical and popular study Bibles. He is author of more than twenty books, including *A Passion for Fullness, The Beauty of Spiritual Language, Rebuilding the Real You*, and *Prayer Is Invading the Impossible*. His musical compositions number over four hundred songs, including the widely sung "Majesty."

About the Writer

JOSEPH SNIDER has worked in Christian ministry for more than twenty years. In addition to freelance writing and speaking, he worked three years with Young Life, served for seven years on the Christian Education faculty at Fort Wayne Bible College, and pastored churches in Indianapolis and Fort Wayne, Indiana. He currently enjoys part-time teaching at Franklin College in Franklin, Indiana. His writing includes material for Thomas Nelson Publishers, Moody Press, Union Gospel Press, and David C. Cook.

Married to Sally Snider, Joe has two grown children, Jenny and Ted. They live in Indianapolis, Indiana. Joe earned a B.A. in English from Cedarville College in Cedarville, Ohio, and a Th.M. in Christian Education from Dallas Theological Seminary.

Of this contributor, the General Editor has remarked: "Joe Snider's strength and stability as a gracious, godly man comes through in his writing. His perceptive and practical way of pointing the way to truth inspires students of God's Word."

THE GIFT
THAT KEEPS ON GIVING

One of the most precious gifts God has given us is His Word, the Bible. Wrapped in the glory and sacrifice of His Son and delivered by the power and ministry of His Spirit, it is a treasured gift—the gift that keeps on giving, because the Giver it reveals is inexhaustible in His love and grace.

Tragically, though, fewer and fewer people are opening this gift and seeking to understand what it's all about and how to use it. They often feel intimidated by it. It requires some assembly, and its instructions are hard to comprehend sometimes. How does the Bible fit together anyway? What does this ancient Book have to say to us who are looking toward the twenty-first century? Will taking the time and energy to understand its instructions and to fit it all together really help you and me?

Yes. Yes. Without a shred of doubt.

The *Spirit-Filled Life® Bible Discovery Guide* series is designed to help you unwrap, assemble, and enjoy all God has for you in the pages of Scripture. It will focus your time and energy on the books of the Bible, the people and places they describe, and the themes and life applications that flow thick from its pages like honey oozing from a beehive.

So you can get the most out of God's Word, this series has a number of helpful features:

 WORD WEALTH

"WORD WEALTH" provides definitions of key terms.

BEHIND THE SCENES

"BEHIND THE SCENES" supplies information about cultural practices, doctrinal disputes, business trades, etc.

 ## AT A GLANCE

"AT A GLANCE" features helpful maps and charts.

 ## BIBLE EXTRA

"BIBLE EXTRA" will guide you to other resources that will enable you to glean more from the Bible's wealth.

 ## PROBING THE DEPTHS

"PROBING THE DEPTHS" will explain controversial issues raised by particular lessons and cite Bible passages and other sources to help you come to your own conclusions.

 ## FAITH ALIVE

The "FAITH ALIVE" feature will help you see and apply the Bible to your day-to-day needs.

The only resources you need to complete and apply these study guides are a heart and mind open to the Holy Spirit, a prayerful attitude, and a pencil and a Bible. Of course, you may draw upon other sources, but these study guides are comprehensive enough to give you all you need to gain a good, basic understanding of the Bible book being covered and how you can apply its themes and counsel to your life.

A word of warning, though. By itself, Bible study will not transform your life. It will not give you power, peace, joy, comfort, hope, and a number of other gifts God longs for you to unwrap and enjoy. Through Bible study, you will grow in your understanding of the Lord, His kingdom and your place in it, but you must be sure to rely on the Holy Spirit to guide your study and your application of the Bible's truths. He, Jesus promised, was sent to teach us "all things" (John 14:26; cf. 1 Cor. 2:13). Bathe your study time in prayer, asking the Spirit of God to illuminate the text, enlighten your mind, humble your will, and comfort your heart. He will never let you down.

My prayer and goal for you is that as you unwrap and begin to explore God's Book for living His way, the Holy Spirit will fill every fiber of your being with the joy and power God longs to give all His children. So read on. Be diligent. Stay open and submissive to Him. You will not be disappointed. He promises you!

Part I:
Our God Is An Awesome God:
Needing the Saving Reign of God
Isaiah 1—39

In the eighth century before Christ, the Chou Dynasty flourished in China, Hindu sages of India started compiling the *Upanishads*, Homer penned the *Iliad* and the *Odyssey* in Greece, and in Judah the prophet Isaiah wrote the most exquisite Hebrew composition of all time. It was an era of high culture in the ancient world.

Isaiah didn't concern himself with art and philosophy. A vision of the holiness of God inspired his genius. Isaiah continues to challenge his readers to see God with the eyes of their hearts and spirits. After we see Him, we see ourselves more clearly than ever before, and we know how much we need the Holy One of Israel to reign in our hearts.

Lesson 1/As the Heart Hardens
Isaiah 1—6

Is Judah cheating on the living God, her Husband of 700 years? Didn't her sister Israel do the same thing and suffer through a messy divorce that left her penniless and stranded in a foreign country?

Who's her latest exotic lover? How jealous is the living God? Did He send a messenger to Judah threatening her with divorce if she didn't break off all her affairs?

Did Judah laugh in the messenger's face and flaunt her latest escapades? Does she think she can get away with it because the living God has put up with her so long?

Is it true that Judah's glamor is wearing thin? That she has to give away more and more to keep the attention of the fast crowd she moves with? What about the rumors that the young nations are about to drop her as soon as they get all her jewels and money?

And who is the mysterious stranger Immanuel? These questions and more are answered in another episode of "As the Heart Hardens."

HOLINESS AND WHOLENESS AT A GLANCE

But first let's remember where our drama comes from. The book of Isaiah is sometimes called a miniature Bible: Sixty-six chapters paralleling sixty-six books. The Bible divides into an Old Testament of thirty-nine books and a New Testament of twenty-seven books. Isaiah breaks into two sections. The first thirty-nine chapters deal with the history of God's people during Isaiah's lifetime. The last twenty-seven chapters begin with a forerunner who will prepare the way for the Messiah, and they end with a description of the new heaven and the new earth.

Isaiah prophesied for about seventy years during the reigns of four kings of Judah (Is. 1:1). List these kings in order below, look up the indicated Scripture, and supply the requested data for each. (Note timeline box on page 14.)

- 1. _____(2 Chr. 26)

Length of reign

Key events of reign

Spiritual tone of reign

- 2. _____(2 Chr. 27)

Length of reign

Key events of reign

Spiritual tone of reign

- 3. _____(2 Chr. 28)

Length of reign

Key events of reign

Spiritual tone of reign

THE LIFE AND TIMES OF ISAIAH THE PROPHET₁

1. Isaiah is born probably during Uzziah's reign.

6. Samaria falls to Assyria (722 B.C.). The northern kingdom goes into exile.

2. Time of increased prosperity in Judah and Israel (Is. 2–4).

7. Philistines invite Hezekiah to ally against Assyria. Isaiah counsels against it (Is. 14:29–32).

8. Hezekiah fortifies his defenses, including construction of a water tunnel (see 2 Chr. 32:30), to resist the Assyrians (Is. 22:8–11).

3. Assyria comes into prominence as a powerful world empire, especially under Tiglath-Pileser III.

9. Sennacherib besieges Jerusalem. Hezekiah prays for deliverance, and Isaiah tells him that God has heard his prayer. When the Lord kills 185,000 Assyrians, the invaders withdraw (Is. 36–37).

4. Isaiah sees a vision of the Lord and is called to minister as a prophet (Is. 6).

10. Hezekiah becomes sick but recovers (Is. 38).

5. Pekah of Israel and Rezin of Damascus rebel against Assyria. They ask Ahaz of Judah to join them, but he refuses (Is. 7).

11. According to tradition, Isaiah is executed during the reign of Manasseh by being sawn in two inside a log.

- 4. _____ (2 Chr. 29–32)

Length of reign

Key events of reign

Spiritual tone of reign

When did Isaiah's prophetic ministry begin? (Is. 6:1)

AT A GLANCE

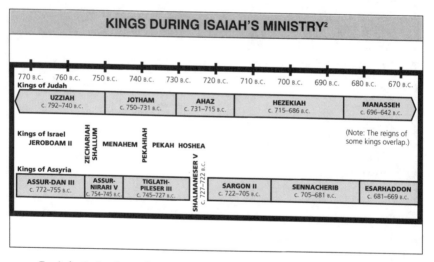

Isaiah 1:2, 3 and 12–20 preview the first thirty-nine chapters of the book. What do you gather are the main ideas of the first portion of Isaiah?

Isaiah 40:9–11 preview the last twenty-seven chapters of the book. What do you gather are the main ideas of the second portion of Isaiah?

There are three dominant ideas in Isaiah. The first appears twenty-six times throughout the prophecies (Is. 1:4; 5:19, 24; 10:20; 12:6; 17:7; 29:19, 23; 30:11, 12, 15; 31:1; 37:23; 41:14, 16, 20; 43:3, 14; 45:11; 47:4; 48:17; 49:7; 54:5; 55:5; 60:9, 14). What is it?

The second dominant idea appears twenty-eight times throughout Isaiah (12:2[2], 3; 17:10; 25:9; 26:1; 33:2, 6; 45:8, 17; 46:13[2]; 49:6, 8; 51:5, 6, 8; 52:7, 10; 56:1; 59:11, 16, 17; 60:18; 61:10; 62:1, 11; 63:5). What is it?

The third major idea of Isaiah's prophecies belongs exclusively to the second part of his book (Is. 41:8, 9; 42:1, 19[2]; 43:10; 44:1, 2, 21[2], 26; 48:20; 49:3, 5–7; 50:10; 52:13; 53:11). What is it?

Weave the three dominant ideas of Isaiah into one sentence as a preview of the whole book of Isaiah. Later you can look back and see how well your sentence fits the book.

ALONG THE WRONG LONGING

The opening sketch of flirty, faithless Judah comes from the reign of Hezekiah when the countryside had been devastated by the Assyrians and Jerusalem nearly besieged (Is. 1:7-9). Isaiah put this late prophecy at the front of the collection because it's a sharp portrait of a hard-hearted, hardheaded people.

In what ways was flirty, faithless Judah like a brood of rebellious children? (Is. 1:2–4)

In what ways was flirty, faithless Judah like someone beaten up by robbers? (Is. 1:5–9)

Flirty, faithless Judah liked to act religiously. What did the Lord think of her religion? (Is. 1:11–15)

How did the Lord advise Judah to deal with her sins? (Is. 1:16–20)

    KINGDOM EXTRA

We may believe that if we sin, we will be immediately aware of it; but sin is subtle, and our hearts may not perceive or acknowledge our guilt. So those most in need of repentance and cleansing may have no awareness of their spiritual state. Therefore, we must continually examine ourselves before the Lord, asking Him to enlighten our hearts to any unacknowledged sin and to cleanse us from all unrighteousness.

When we disagree with God's agenda, we must repent and change our way of thinking (Is. 1:16, 17). Repentance and obedience are reasonable to a willing and obedient heart, but folly to one with a resistant and rebellious attitude (vv. 18-20).[3]

Why do you think Isaiah compared Judah to Sodom and Gomorrah and to a prostitute? (Is. 1:9, 10, 21–24)

How did the Lord propose dealing with the sin of flirty, faithless Judah? (Is. 1:24–31)

 WORD WEALTH

A **terebinth tree** (Is. 1:29, 30) is a spreading tree with reddish-green leaves and clusters of red berries. It grows to a height of twenty to twenty-five feet. The seasonal dormancy and reawakening of the terebinth made it suitable as a sacred tree for fertility cults. The **gardens** may be groves of sacred terebinth where both Baal and his consort Ashtaroth were worshiped with immoral rituals.

STUMBLING IN THE DARK

Both Old and New Testaments use the imagery of walking in the light and in the dark to illustrate the benefits of obeying God and the consequences of disobeying Him. Not surprisingly, flirty, faithless Judah preferred partying in the dark because her "deeds were evil" (John 3:19).

When Isaiah looked ahead under the leadership of the Spirit of God, how did he see Judah walking in the distant future? (Is. 2:1–4)

Not quite so far into the future the prophet saw the Lord purging Judah of sin so she would walk in the light. How did he describe this purging?

- The problem (Is. 2:5–9)

- The remedy (Is. 2:10–19)

- The result (Is. 2:20–22)

From Isaiah 3:1–15, list as many complaints as you can that the Lord made against the leaders who caused Judah to stumble in the darkness of disobedience.

Try to picture the imaginary woman Isaiah described in 3:16, 18–23. What did flirty, faithless Judah look like as she partied in the dark? (Is. 3:16, 18–23)

Describe the calamity that awaited foolish, promiscuous Judah (Is. 3:17, 24—4:1)

FAITH ALIVE

Apply the imagery of Isaiah 2:16—4:1 to a sin you struggle with in your life. How is yielding to this temptation like being a silly floozy partying in the dark?

•

How could the consequences of walking in the dark of this sin bring judgment on your life?

A GOOD BRANCH IN A ROTTEN VINEYARD

The Lord had entered a covenant with His people that could be likened to a marriage. Isaiah pictured Judah, the Lord's bride, as a lovely vineyard. He saw her under a wedding canopy (Is. 4:6). He sang a love ballad about the Lord and His vineyard bride (5:1, 2). But the ballad ended on a note of discord. The bride wasn't content with her Groom.

Isaiah 4:2 continues the theme of judgment present in verse 1 as marked by the phrase "in that day" introducing both verses. God's judgment on His people ultimately is restorative. What blessings will follow the calamities awaiting flirty, faithless Judah? (Is. 4:2–6)

BIBLE EXTRA

The Branch of the Lord first appears in Isaiah 4:2 as a messianic figure of speech. What is revealed about the Messiah in each of these Branch passages?
• Isaiah 4:2

- Isaiah 11:1, 10

- Jeremiah 23:5, 6; 33:15, 16

- Zechariah 3:8–10

- Zechariah 6:12, 13

Isaiah 5:1–7 steps back from the future to the prophet's day and elaborates the metaphor of Judah as a vineyard. Summarize the various portions of this metaphor.

- Description of the vineyard (Is. 5:1, 2)

- Owner's intentions for the vineyard (Is. 5:3–6)

- Application to Judah (Is. 5:7)

 FAITH ALIVE

Much of the rest of Isaiah 5 contains a list of woes that expands the idea of oppression and unrighteousness introduced in verse 7. Identify the sins condemned in these woes and describe how they express themselves in modern life? (The first sin is identified for you as an example)

- Isaiah 5:8–10 — Greed

- Isaiah 5:11, 12 — _____

- Isaiah 5:18, 19 — _____

- Isaiah 5:20, 21 — _____

- Isaiah 5:22, 23 — _____

The last verses of Isaiah 5 describe the imminent judgment flirty, faithless Judah faced. Summarize the two ways Isaiah presented this punishment.
- Using the vineyard metaphor (Is. 5:24, 25)

- Describing the Assyrian army (Is. 5:26–30)

CURE FOR A HARD HEART

Isaiah knew he was part of the flirty, faithless nation of Judah. He had pronounced several woes against the nation (Is. 5:8–23), but he saved the last woe to proclaim against himself (Is. 6:5). Because he was part of Judah, Isaiah could present his own experience as a guide to his countrymen in becoming a tender-hearted, faithful bride to the Lord.

Describe the vision of the Lord Isaiah had in the year King Uzziah died. (Is. 6:1–4)

 KINGDOM EXTRA

The ministry of the seraphim is closely related to the throne and the praises of God. They are seen constantly glorifying God — extolling His nature and attributes, and apparently supervising heaven's worship. It is possible the seraphim are the praising angels of Psalm 148:2 though they are not specifically identified as such. Whereas cherubim are positioned beside and around the throne of God (Ps. 9:1; Rev. 4:6), the six-winged seraphim are seen as hovering above the throne as they minister in worship.[4]

How did Isaiah's encounter with God reveal to him his deepest spiritual need and then resolve that need? (Is. 6:5–7)

How did Isaiah's encounter with the Lord prepare him for his prophetic ministry? (Is. 6:8)

How did the Lord describe Isaiah's ministry to him?
• In terms of its effectiveness (Is. 6:9, 10)

• In terms of its duration (Is. 6:11–13)

 FAITH ALIVE

How does each new insight you receive into the holiness and character of God reveal your own need for new spiritual cleansing and renewal?

How does each new insight you receive into the holiness and character of God prepare you to handle greater ministry responsibilities?

1. *The Word in Life Study Bible* (Nashville, Thomas Nelson, 1996), 1154, "The Life and Times of Isaiah the Prophet."
2. Ibid., 1154.
3. *Spirit-Filled Life® Bible* (Nashville: Thomas Nelson, 1991), 1051, "Truth-in-Action through Isaiah."
4. Ibid., 969, "Kingdom Dynamics: Is. 6:2, Seraphim."

Lesson 2/O Come, O Come, Immanuel
Isaiah 1—12

We are fascinated with historical accounts of children who became kings. Tutankhamen was eight or nine years old when he became pharaoh of Egypt. Joash was seven when he assumed the throne of David in Judah. Alexander was twenty when he first sat on the throne of Macedonia and started to become great. Frederick II was King of Sicily at four and Holy Roman Emperor at eighteen. Louis IV became King of France when he was thirteen.

Most of these young rulers had regents who administered their government until they grew older, but the idea of a child-king continues to exert a tug on our imaginations. We think a child-king would play fair and, therefore, be just. We think he would tell the truth and keep his word. We think he would be honorable with noble people and humble with ordinary folk. We think he would be unspoiled by the cynicism and lust for power that stains the pages of political history.

Child-kings belong to fairy tales where they represent the ideals of an imaginary world. But *the* Child-King belongs to the pages of biblical prophecy where He promises to bring the Kingdom of God to earth at the end of time. In Isaiah 4:2 the prophet introduces a mysterious figure called "the Branch of the Lord," who will bring in an age of flourishing fruitfulness to God's people. In chapter 11:1 Isaiah reveals that the Branch of the Lord is also the Child-King.

The Child-King's name is Immanuel—"God with us." Why would God picture His reign on earth in terms of a Child-King?

SAVE US FROM CALAMITY

Isaiah liked to introduce his messianic titles mysteriously. The first mention of the Branch, the Child, or the Servant is vague, the next perhaps ambiguous, and the ensuing ones increasingly clear. Not surprisingly, the Child appears like "a riddle wrapped in an enigma," as the saying goes. And He makes His entrance in between Isaiah's sons with the tongue-twisting names. One thing was crystal clear. The Child would save His people from disaster.

As many as ten years passed between Uzziah's death mentioned in Isaiah 6:1 and "the days of Ahaz the son of Jotham, the son of Uzziah" (7:1). The unbelief that God had said would characterize Judah's response to Isaiah's ministry (6:9, 10) had begun to express itself.

What was the political and religious situation when King Ahaz began his reign? (Is. 7:1, 2; see 2 Kin. 16:1–6)

How did the Lord advise King Ahaz about Israel and Syria through Isaiah the prophet? (Is. 7:3–9)

How did King Ahaz try to make himself appear humble and spiritual? (Is. 7:10–12)

What was King Ahaz's real reason for avoiding the will of God? (see 2 Kin. 16:7–9)

What were the spiritual consequences of Ahaz's indifference to the will of God? (see 2 Kin. 16:10–16)

What was the Lord's response to king Ahaz's false piety? (Is. 7:13, 14)

The prophecy of Immanuel's birth causes Christians to jump ahead seven centuries in their thoughts to the birth of Jesus, but the prophecy had to refer as well to another less spectacular birth in the days of King Ahaz. If the king had paid attention to the Lord, what would he have looked for?

- In terms of the birth? (Is. 7:14)

- In terms of the child's name? (Is. 7:14)

- In terms of the time before God's deliverance would come? (Is. 7:15, 16)

  BIBLE EXTRA

The prophecy of the Virgin Birth has been a source of considerable controversy due to the use of the Hebrew word 'almah, which can be translated "young woman," as well as "virgin." The Lord was giving the sign of a child to King Ahaz, and the conception of that child is recorded in chapter 8. But the Holy Spirit also was speaking of the birth of the Messiah who would come, and that Child would literally be born of a virgin. The fact that Christ was virgin-born is indisputable from Matthew and Luke's use of the Greek word *parthenos,* which definitely means "virgin" (Matt. 1:23; Luke 1:27).[1]

What price would King Ahaz and the kingdom of Judah pay for rejecting the counsel of the Lord? (Is. 7:18–25)

Isaiah had two sons whose names were perpetual prophecies to the leaders and people of Judah. The first son was Shear-Jashub, whom Isaiah took with him as an object lesson when he told Ahaz that the Lord would break the power of Israel and Syria (Is. 7:3). Isaiah wrote the name of his second son, Maher-Shalal-Hash-Baz on a huge notarized scroll that could be mounted in a public place where passersby could see it (8:1, 2).

Shear-Jashub meant "A Remnant Shall Return." What do you think that name predicted for Judah?

Maher-Shalal-Hash-Baz meant "Speed the Spoil, Hasten the Booty." What was Judah to learn from this name? (Is. 8:3, 4)

How did the Lord summarize the situation Judah faced with the Assyrian Empire?
- The danger (Is. 8:5–8a)

- The Savior (Is. 8:8b, 10b)

- Assyria's future (Is. 8:9, 10a)

In the face of the Assyrian threat, how did the Lord want His people to respond?
- To the danger (Is. 8:12)

- To the Lord (Is. 8:13–15)

- To fellow believers (Is. 8:16–18)

 BIBLE EXTRA

"A stone of stumbling and a rock of offense" (Is. 8:14) describes God in language that occurs in other key Bible passages. Look up each of the following, and write what the language about a (corner) stone describes. Write enough that will remind you at a glance of what is in each passage.

Psalm 118:21–23

Daniel 2:34, 44–45

Matthew 21:33–45

Acts 4:8–12

Ephesians 2:19–22

1 Peter 2:4–8

WORD WEALTH

Fear (Is. 8:13) translates a Hebrew word that occurs a dozen times in the Old Testament, beginning at Genesis 9:2 which speaks of the dread Noah's descendants would inspire in all the animals after the Flood. Psalm 76:11 says that the Lord "ought to be feared." People should not live in dread or terror of God as though He were an arbitrary despot. He is to be feared because He is all-powerful and He is unspeakably holy. In the present reference, Isaiah is admonished *by the Lord Himself* never to fear human threats, but to let God alone be the object of his reverential fear.[2]

BIBLE EXTRA

Messiah's Patient Wait (Is. 8:17, 18). While many biblical interpreters limit the meaning of "I and the children whom the Lord has given me" to the prophet and his sons, the writer of Hebrews interprets them as words of the Messiah (Heb. 2:13). Jesus identified Himself with all Christians as His spiritual children and indicates that we will be signs and wonders to the world as the Second Coming approaches.[3]

SAVE US FROM PRIDE

When Assyria first began to conquer Israel to the north of Judah, the kingdom of Israel was so self-confident that the people figured they would take advantage of the devastation of war to build better cities and plant better forests (Is. 9:8–10). In time the proud people would face their disgrace. Was there any hope for them? Yes. In the future the Child-King would come first to the battered frontiers of Israel to become the Prince of Peace.

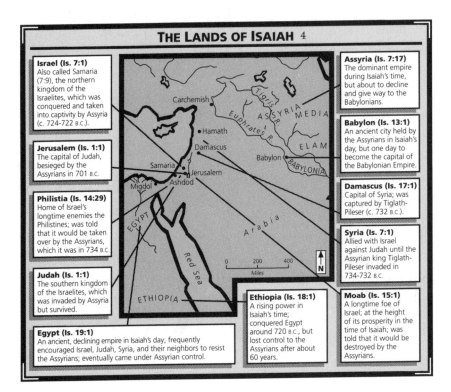

THE LANDS OF ISAIAH 4

Israel (Is. 7:1)
Also called Samaria (7:9), the northern kingdom of the Israelites, which was conquered and taken into captivity by Assyria (c. 724-722 B.C.).

Jerusalem (Is. 1:1)
The capital of Judah, besieged by the Assyrians in 701 B.C.

Philistia (Is. 14:29)
Home of Israel's longtime enemies the Philistines; was told that it would be taken over by the Assyrians, which it was in 734 B.C.

Judah (Is. 1:1)
The southern kingdom of the Israelites, which was invaded by Assyria but survived.

Egypt (Is. 19:1)
An ancient, declining empire in Isaiah's day; frequently encouraged Israel, Judah, Syria, and their neighbors to resist the Assyrians; eventually came under Assyrian control.

Assyria (Is. 7:17)
The dominant empire during Isaiah's time, but about to decline and give way to the Babylonians.

Babylon (Is. 13:1)
An ancient city held by the Assyrians in Isaiah's day, but one day to become the capital of the Babylonian Empire.

Damascus (Is. 17:1)
Capital of Syria; was captured by Tiglath-Pileser (c. 732 B.C.).

Syria (Is. 7:1)
Allied with Israel against Judah until the Assyrian king Tiglath-Pileser invaded in 734-732 B.C.

Ethiopia (Is. 18:1)
A rising power in Isaiah's time; conquered Egypt around 720 B.C., but lost control to the Assyrians after about 60 years.

Moab (Is. 15:1)
A longtime foe of Israel; at the height of its prosperity in the time of Isaiah; was told that it would be destroyed by the Assyrians.

Map labels: Carchemish, Hamath, Damascus, Samaria, Jerusalem, Migdol, Ashdod, Babylon, Euphrates R., Tigris R., ASSYRIA, MEDIA, ELAM, BABYLONIA, EGYPT, Arabia, Red Sea, ETHIOPIA

0   200   400
Miles

In summary, how would the proud northern Israelites act when the Assyrians conquered them? (Is. 8:19–22)

What did the Lord desire for these border people who took the brunt of the Assyrian assault? (Is. 9:1, 2)

What destiny had the Lord prepared for the Assyrian conquerors? (Is. 9:3–5)

The permanent solution to the idolatry that resulted in judgment and to the cruelty of conquerors like Assyria can only be found in God's Child-King. What is suggested to you about the Child-King by His various names? (Is. 9:6)

- Child

- Son

- Wonderful Counselor

- Mighty God

- Everlasting Father (literally, "Father of eternity")

- Prince of Peace

What will the Child-King's government be like? (Is. 9:7)

KINGDOM EXTRA

In Isaiah 9:6 we have one of the most beautifully poetic promises of the Messiah's coming reign. Yearly we recite this verse and hear it sung as we celebrate Christmas. Yet this verse also contains a reference to one of the great, incomprehensible truths in the Bible: the Incarnation—"a Child is born . . . a Son is given."

God would become a man. A newborn baby would be called "Mighty God, Everlasting Father." We can accept that truth by faith, but we cannot fully grasp what it meant for the Second Person of the Godhead to shed His eternal state and put on flesh. But Paul tells us that He took the form of a servant and became as a man. "Therefore God also has highly exalted Him and given Him the name which is above every name" (Phil. 2:7).[4]

In Isaiah's day, the proud kingdom of Israel (Is. 9:9) was not ready to respond to the Child-King. It would be seven centuries before the prediction of Isaiah 9:1, 2 began to be fulfilled in the earthly ministry of Jesus (Matt. 4:13–17). What fate awaited various people in proud rebellious Israel? (Is. 9:13–17)

- Leaders

- Prophets

- Strong young men

- Helpless widows and orphans

What would happen to the unity of proud Israel in the face of the judgment of God? (Is. 9:18–21)

Proud Israel did not want to be saved by the Child-King. Describe the woe that faced her.

• Her sins (Is. 10:1, 2)

• Her stubbornness (Is. 10:3, 4)

• Her judgment (Is. 9:12b, 17b, 21b; 10:4b)

SAVE US BY THE SPIRIT OF WISDOM

This is the first prolonged passage of hope for the distant future in Isaiah. The Child-King is once more called the Branch (11:1), and He is linked for the first time with the Spirit of God who inspires the Branch-Child-King with the qualities that will make His kingdom rule the end of all oppression (v. 2).

Before looking far into the future, Isaiah looked at Assyria's near future. How did the Lord and Assyria view the cruel empire's conquests?

• The Lord's view (Is. 10:5, 6)

• Assyria's view (Is. 10:7–11)

What future did the cruel Assyrian Empire face at the hand of God? (Is. 10:12–19)

How does Isaiah 10:20–23 fulfill the name of Isaiah's first son, Shear-Jashub, A Remnant Shall Return?

What message did Isaiah want the Southern Kingdom of Judah to learn from the events that faced the Northern Kingdom of Israel? (Is. 10:24–34)

The Lord would cut down the forest of the mighty Assyrian army (Is. 10:33, 34). He does not express His glory through impressive human agencies. He prefers to glorify Himself through the weak and despised things of this world (1 Cor. 1:26–31). How does the Branch from the stem of Jesse (King David's father) fit this pattern? (Is. 11:1)

What do you think the different names for the Spirit of the Lord reveal about the ministry of the Spirit in the life of the Branch? (Is. 11:2)

• The Spirit of wisdom and understanding

• The Spirit of counsel and might

• The Spirit of knowledge and of the fear of the Lord

 BIBLE EXTRA

The Holy Spirit is mentioned specifically fifteen times in the book of Isaiah, not counting references to the Spirit's power, effect, or influence apart from the mention of His name. There are three general categories under which the work of the Holy Spirit may be described:

1. The Spirit's anointing upon the Messiah to empower Him for His rule and administration as King on the throne of David (11:1–12); as the suffering Servant of the Lord who will heal, liberate, enlighten, and bring justice to the nations (42:1–9); as the Anointed One (Messiah) in both His advents (61:1–3; Luke 4:17–21).

2. The Spirit's outpouring upon Israel to give them success in their rehabilitation after the pattern of the Exodus (44:1–5; 63:1–5); to protect them from their enemies (59:19); and to preserve Israel in covenant relationship with Yahweh (59:21). However, Israel must be careful not to rebel and grieve the Holy Spirit (63:10; Eph. 4:30).

3. The Spirit's operation at creation and in the preservation of nature (40:13; *see* also 48:16).

The Lord Jesus, whose earthly ministry was carried out in the power and anointing of the Holy Spirit, as Isaiah had prophesied, promised to pour out His Spirit upon the church to empower it for its ministry in fulfilling the Great Commission.[5]

What qualities of the ministry of the Branch from the stem of Jesse will save us from oppression? (Is. 11:3–5)

BIBLE EXTRA

"**The Spirit of the Lord shall rest upon Him**" (11:1–3). The coming Davidic ruler, whose name is Immanuel (7:14), will judge the people with righteousness and fairness (11:3–5), by bearing the effectual qualities of the Spirit's work in His ministry—"wisdom, understanding, counsel, might, knowledge, and the fear of the Lord (v. 2). All these expressions of the Spirit were present within Jesus' life for anointed ministry (Luke 4:14), for "God was with Him" (*see* Acts 10:38). When we receive the Spirit's fullness, Jesus' life becomes alive in us—God is with us—and His ruling authority flows through us in multiplied ministries and gifts (1 Cor. 12:4–11).[6]

How will the reign of the Branch from the stem of Jesse affect the following?
- The effects of human sin on the animal creation (Is. 11:6–9)

- The gentile nations (Is. 11:10)

- The scattered people of Israel and Judah (Is. 11:11–16)

Isaiah 12 consists of a psalm of praise from the perspective of God's people delivered from oppression. How do they praise Him?
- Among themselves (Is. 12:1–3)

- To other people (Is. 12:4–6)

WORD WEALTH

Yah is the shorter form of the Lord's holy name *Yahweh*, or Jehovah. This contracted form of the name of the Lord God appears fifty times in the Old Testament. Forty-four occur in Psalms, and the other six are in Exodus and Isaiah. Many references in the Psalms involve the compound word *Hallelu-Yah*, which literally means "You must all praise Yah!" This word has spread from Hebrew into many languages and is a beautiful expression suitable for joyous worship.[7]

FAITH ALIVE

In your Christian experience, how has the Lord Jesus been gentle and humble with you like a Child-King?

How has Immanuel rescued you from calamity in the course of your life?

How has He opposed pride in your personality and worked to root it out?

How has the Lord's Branch freed you from the oppression of the world, the flesh, or the devil?

1. "Messianic Promises," *Hayford's Bible Handbook* (Nashville: Thomas Nelson, 1995), 701.

2. *Spirit-Filled Life® Bible* (Nashville: Thomas Nelson, 1991), 973, "Word Wealth: Is. 8:13, fear."

3. James Smith, *What the Bible Teaches about the Promised Messiah* (Nashville: Thomas Nelson, 1993), 260.

4. *The Word In Life™ Study Bible* (Nashville: Thomas Nelson, 1996), 1150, "The Lands of Isaiah."

5. *Spirit-Filled Life® Bible*, 974, "Kingdom Dynamics: Is. 9:6, Messiah's Becoming a Man."

6. *Hayford's Bible Handbook*, 172.

7. *Spirit-Filled Life® Bible*, "Kingdom Life Insight, Is. 11:1–3."

8. Ibid., 979, "Word Wealth: Is. 12:2, Yah."

Lesson 3/All The Nations Are His
Isaiah 13—23

On a cold December night, a pioneer traveler emerged from the forest in the upper reaches of the Mississippi River. Light was fading, the air was bitterly cold, and the only town for days was on the other side. No open water showed in either direction as far as the traveler could see, but he had no idea if the ice would support him.

The man walked out from shore on the ice. Twenty yards from land, the color of the ice changed and he got down on his hands and knees to distribute his weight more widely. As he approached the midpoint of his crossing, the man strained his ears for any sound that might signal weak ice. His heart froze as he heard something, but it sounded like singing. Louder and louder the song grew, accompanied by the crunch of hooves on the ice. A farm wagon on runners loomed out of the dark at a trot and glided past the crawling traveler.

The man felt a proper fool crawling in terror across ice that would hold up a caroling farmer, a workhorse, a wagon, and a winter's supply of coal. He jumped to his feet and hurried to the west bank without another anxious thought about the ice that suddenly seemed as solid as the ground he had walked on all day.

The people of the little nation of Judah were tempted to worry that God's authority might collapse if He had to contend with the gods, kings, and armies of powerful lands. In fact they could trust Him as surely as the farmer with his coal trusted the ice on the Mississippi.

GOD CONTROLS SUPERPOWERS

Isaiah's prophecies concerning the nations of his day extend from chapter 13 through 23. The first and last prophecies of this section—the "bookends" of these chapters—concern superpowers, one political and the other economic. In between Isaiah dealt with other nations—big and small, famous and obscure. If God controls the superpowers, the other should be no problem. (See map, "The Lands of Isaiah," in Lesson 1.)

Who was the political superpower and what was its destiny? (13:1, 19)

Summarize the judgment God had in store for the political superpower. (Is. 13:17–22)

Which aspects of Isaiah's message of judgment upon Babylon foreshadow God's final judgment of evil upon the earth in the last days? (Is. 13:2–16; Matt. 24:29)

What fate awaited the king of dreaded Babylon? (Is. 14:1–11, 16–21)

BIBLE EXTRA

Isaiah 14:12–15 has a double application. These verses are still part of the proverb against the king of Babylon. The language, however, shows that he is a type, or symbol, of Satan. Lucifer means "Light Bearer."[1]

What does the beginning and end of the passage tell you about the past, present, and future of Satan? (Is. 14:12, 15)

- Past

- Present

- Future

What do the five "I will" statements reveal about Satan's character? (Is 14:13, 14)

KINGDOM EXTRA

Humility is essential to righteous, Christ-like behavior. Humility and meekness are Spirit-engendered characteristics in the mature believer. Their opposites, pride and arrogance, have a diabolical source. Humility refuses to promote its own interests, but looks out, rather, for the interests of others.

Beware of selfish ambition that sets itself above God and pride that takes glory from God. Understand that they are the hallmarks of Satan's rebellion through which he became God's enemy.[2]

When Isaiah wrote about Babylon, it had not yet risen to replace Assyria as the power in Mesopotamia. As he concluded his prophecy about the political superpower, Isaiah rolled Babylon and Assyria together in a concluding statement of doom. What guarantees did Isaiah give that his predictions would come true? (Is. 14:22–27)

BIBLE EXTRA

Tyre, a seaport, is another name for Phoenicia, the leading maritime power of Isaiah's day. Its empire extended as far as the coast of North Africa, perhaps even to Spain. Phoenicians invented the alphabet, evidence of an advanced civilization; however, their religion was abominable. They worshiped Baal and Ashteroth, the deities that the Tyrian Jezebel brought into Israel, and which Elijah withstood and humiliated on Mt. Carmel.[3]

What would be the reaction of the entire Mediterranean world to the fall of Tyre? (Is. 23:1–7)

Why did the Lord decide to bring judgment on the economic superpower Tyre? (Is. 23:8–12)

What did Isaiah predict as the final relationship between Judah, the people of God, and Babylon, the political superpower? (Is. 14:1, 2)

What did Isaiah predict as the final relationship between Judah, the people of God, and Tyre, the economic superpower? (Is. 23:15–18)

 FAITH ALIVE

Which superpowers of the world are you tempted to worry about?
• Political

• Economic

How do you think God wants you to react to these superpowers?

GOD CONTROLS TERRORISTS

Judah was a small country surrounded by other small nations. One of the realities of Near Eastern politics was the eagerness of these small states to take advantage of Judah's troubles by launching quick strikes to weaken this strange nation that didn't have a visible god.

The five Philistine cities had been Israel's enemy along the Mediterranean coast since the days of Samson. What was the Lord's message to Philistia for celebrating when Judah had to pay tribute to Assyria? (Is. 14:28–32)

Moab was a small country east of the Dead Sea. The Moabites were descendants of Lot's incestuous relationship with his older daughter (Gen. 19:30-38). Isaiah devoted a great deal of space to the fate of this nation. What is said about Moab also applies to the other terrorist nations.

How would the citizens of Moab react to the judgment God sent on them in the form of an invading army? (Is. 15:1–4; 16:12)

Why did the Lord judge the terrorist nation Moab so severely? (Is. 16:6)

How did the Lord judge Moab? (Is. 15:6–9; 16:8, 14)

What was Isaiah's reaction to the horrible suffering in Moab caused by the judgment of God on their sin? (Is. 15:5; 16:9–11)

Moab had tried to weaken and harm Judah. What would Moab have to do in order for her refugees to survive? (Is. 16:1–5)

    BIBLE EXTRA

Jerusalem's Ideal King (Is. 16:6). The leaders of Moab conclude that their only salvation is found in the Davidic dynasty ruling from Zion. The Son of David [the Messiah] now rules the earth, and the defeated Moabites recognize Him as their king. The lamb is sent from Sela (Petra) in Edom where the Moabites have fled for refuge. He who will occupy that throne will rule in truth.[4]

Syria to the northeast and Israel to the north of Judah had allied themselves to wear Judah down with constant border skirmishes. God lumped Israel right in with the gentile Syrians because they had become terrorists against the Davidic dynasty in Jerusalem.

What did Isaiah predict about Syria and Israel in each of these areas of national life?

- Military strength (Is. 17:1–3)

- Economic prosperity (Is. 17:4–6)

- Idolatry (Is. 17:7, 8)

- The future (Is. 17:9–11)

Because this judgment included Israel, the Lord predicted through Isaiah the fate of the Assyrians who would do Israel so much harm. What fate awaited the Assyrians? (Is. 17:12–14)

To the south and east of God's people were Edom and the Arabian tribes, two more small nomadic peoples who hated Judah and who were renowned as desert caravan raiders. How did these terrorists cope with the constant danger around them? (Is. 21:11, 12)

What fate awaited these people known for their violence and daring? (Is. 21:13–17)

FAITH ALIVE

Terrorism is a growing threat around the world. No place can regard itself as immune from the cowardly but lethal strikes of fanatical groups that are too small to engage in frontal attacks on those they hate.

What terrorist groups are you tempted to worry about?

What do you think God wants your attitude to be toward terrorists? Why?

GOD CONTROLS ANCIENT CULTURES

In every age certain ancient cultures exert an influence far beyond the political and military might of their countries. They are the source of philosophies, literature, political systems, religions, and educational theories that influence everyone around them.

How can you tell the ancient culture of Ethiopia was held in high esteem by the rest of the nations? (Is. 18:1, 2, 7)

How did the Lord describe the defeat of this ancient and powerful civilization? (Is. 18:3–6)

How would the judgment on Egypt work itself out?
* In the religion of Egypt (Is. 19:1)

* In the unity of Egypt (Is. 19:2–4)

* In the climate of Egypt (Is. 19:5–10)

* In the leadership of Egypt (Is. 19:11–17)

How did Isaiah illustrate the judgment hanging over the heads of the ancient cultures of Ethiopia and Egypt? (Is. 20:1–6)

What unexpected future awaits the ancient culture Egypt, the terrorist nation Israel, and the superpower Assyria? (Is. 19:18–25)

There were other ancient cultures in the Near East which Assyria would conquer. How did Isaiah describe these?
* Assyria, Elam, and Media's defeat of Babylon between 710 and 703 B.C. (Is. 21:1, 2)

* Judah's reaction to ancient Babylon's surrender to Assyria (Is. 21:3–10)

* Ancient Judah's reaction when Assyria would attack them (Is. 22:1–4)

* Jerusalem's defense when the armies of Assyria and its allies besieged her (Is. 22:5–11)

After the Assyrian army was struck down by God (Is. 37:36–38), what reactions did Isaiah record?

- Judah's proper reaction (Is. 22:12)

- Judah's actual reaction (Is. 22:13)

- The Lord's reaction (Is. 22:14)

How do Greek, Roman, and more recent European cultures continue to influence our lives?

FAITH ALIVE

What non-Christian ideas grow out of these ancient cultures and trouble God's people?

How do you think God wants you to regard these ancient cultures? Why?

GOD EVEN CONTROLS TRAITORS

Isaiah's prophecies about the nations were interrupted by two personal messages to government officials of Judah who had abused their offices. They were traitors, each in his unique way. Traitors can be as dangerous as rogue nations or terrorist organizations.

What did Shebna do that offended God? (Is. 22:15, 16)

How was Shebna's sin like the sin of others in this portion of Isaiah? (14:13, 14; 16:6)

How did the Lord's punishment fit Shebna's crime? (Is. 22:17–19)

How did Eliakim serve the government of Judah better than Shebna had? (Is. 22:20–23)

Although Eliakim served his government well, he ghost-employed most of his family (Is. 22:24). How did the Lord deal with Eliakim? (Is. 22:25)

 FAITH ALIVE

What do you think is the solution to corruption among government officials?

What do you think God wants His church to do about corruption in government?

1. *Spirit-Filled Life® Bible* (Nashville: Thomas Nelson, 1991), 981, note on Is. 14:12–21.

2. Ibid., 1051, "Truth-in-Action through Isaiah."

3. Ibid., 990, note on Is. 23:1–18.

4. James Smith, *What the Bible Teaches About the Promised Messiah* (Nashville: Thomas Nelson, 1993), 277, 278.

Lesson 4/All's Well That Ends Well
Isaiah 24—27

"All's Well That Ends Well" is the title of Shakespeare's naughty little soap opera. Helena, the virtuous daughter of a recently deceased doctor, loves the nobleman Bertram. Using her father's remedies, Helena cures the King of France, who orders Bertram to wed her. Evil Parolles convinces Bertram that Helena is unworthy of his love, and the shenanigans begin.

With more tricks and twists than an "I Love Lucy" episode, Shakespeare brings Helena and Bertram together and punishes Parolles. At times it seems impossible. Audiences pull for Helena and despise Parolles but scarcely dare hope she will prevail.

As children we wanted things to come out right. We played games by the rules because it only felt right to win fairly. We read stories expecting the good guys to win and the bad guys to lose. If the game board looked wrong at the end or the story left the hero in trouble, we were unhappy.

We want life to turn out fairly inside the framework of our earthly lives. But God's game board and the plot of God's story reach way beyond any one person's life. Consistently, however, the Bible solemnly promises, as does Shakespeare's silly little play, "All's Well That Ends Well."

GOD WILL JUDGE THE WHOLE WORLD

After Isaiah finished his messages of judgment on the nations of his day, he penned a prophetic panorama of the last days that prefigured the apocalyptic visions of Ezekiel, Daniel, Zechariah, and the apostle John. The theme of judgment continues to dominate chapter 24, but the whole earth is in view and the time frame has dropped from view.

The prophet began with a general statement of judgment on the world and all its people. What did Isaiah say about

- The earth? (Is. 24:1)

- The world population? (Is. 24:2)

- Inhabited lands? (Is. 24:3)

What effect does the sinfulness of mankind have on the physical world we live in? (Is. 24:4–6)

What "laws," "ordinance," and "everlasting covenant" do you think God holds all humans of all times accountable for? (Is. 24:5)

What is the symbol Isaiah used through these chapters for organized evil? (Is. 24:10, 12; 25:2, 3; 26:5)

What are the symbols Isaiah used in these chapters to designate organized righteousness? (Is. 25:6, 7, 10; 26:1, 2)

What will be the first signs that the judgment of God has finally come upon the evil world system? (Is. 24:7–12)

What will be the response of the righteous remnant that survives the Lord's judgment on the city of the evil world system? (Is. 24:13–16a)

What will be some of the dreadful terrors that await the wicked who undergo the judgment on the city of the evil world system? (Is. 24:16b–20)

How did Isaiah summarize the ultimate destinies of the wicked and the righteous? (Is. 24:21–23)

 KINGDOM EXTRA

"In that day . . . the Lord will punish on high the host of exalted ones" (Is. 24:21). The spiritual war is brought to the forefront in this verse. The present application of the prophetic significance is best seen through the pen of Paul in 2 Corinthians 10:5. The day Isaiah wrote of prophetically applies to "today" when all hell appears to be breaking loose around us. At these times, [spiritual] warfare requires a confronting and casting down of the enemy when it exalts itself against the Most High God. Our boldness will come from realizing that God Himself will punish the enemy.[1]

FAITH ALIVE

What are some of the sins and injustices that you will be happy to see put right when the Lord finally judges the whole world?

How do you think you should respond to sin and injustice in the world today in light of God's future judgment of the whole world? Why do you believe this?

VISIONS OF THE KINGDOM: THE GLORY OF FINAL JUSTICE

Chapter 25 of Isaiah contains a psalm of personal praise to God inspired by the prophet's vision of final justice. Isaiah 24 emphasized the universality of final judgment on wickedness; chapter 25 stresses the universality of final blessing on His people, whatever their nationality, when God's Kingdom has conquered all evil and is nowhere resisted. We can find ourselves in the poetry of this eighth-century B.C. Hebrew prophet.

For what things did Isaiah praise the Lord concerning His future judgment on the city of organized evil? (Is. 25:1–5)

For what things did Isaiah praise the Lord concerning His future blessing on the mountain, representing the complete, public establishment of God's Kingdom? (Is. 25:6–9) [Assume that "the covering" and "the veil" (v. 7) are the same as "death" (v. 8)].

BIBLE EXTRA

Isaiah's praise of God for His future conquest of death and its associated sorrow inspired other biblical writers. Paul alluded to the first part of verse 8 when he wrote, "Death is swallowed up in victory" (1 Cor. 15:54). John had the last part of verse 8 in mind when he wrote, "And God will wipe away every tear from their eyes; there shall be no more death, nor sorrow, nor crying. There shall be no more pain, for the former things have passed away" (Rev. 21:4, see 7:17).

Think about the ministry of Jesus, about His raising people from the dead (the daughter of Jarius, Mark 5:21–43, and Lazarus, John 11) and about His own resurrection. In what way is the prophecy of Isaiah fulfilled in the ministry of Jesus?

See Matthew 3:2 and 4:17, along with 12:28. What do these verses suggest regarding the kingdom of God prophesied by Isaiah in this chapter?

If we grant that the kingdom of God dawned in the ministry of Jesus, what is the status of the kingdom of God today? How are we to explain the presence of God's kingdom when not every prophecy concerning it has been completely fulfilled?

For some reason Isaiah attached a lot of importance to Moab as an enemy of Judah, the people of God (Is. 15—16). In Isaiah 25:10, the prophet used the name Moab as equivalent to "the city," a symbol for all the organized evil of the world. While the mountain of God will be secure under God's hand, how will God's hands and feet be employed against wickedness? (Is. 25:10–12)

FAITH ALIVE

Some people think that looking to the future for ultimate blessing and justice instead of insisting on it in this life is nothing more than "pie in the sky by-and-by." How do you respond to that criticism?

Write a prayer or psalm of praise to God expressing the things you are grateful for or excited about as you contemplate the final justice He extends to the righteous and the wicked.

VISIONS OF THE KINGDOM:
THE GLORY OF FINAL SALVATION

The psalm in Isaiah 25 was sung in the first person singular "I." The song of Isaiah 26 is sung in the first person plural, "we." The singers are the redeemed remnant of Israel, "the righteous nation" (v. 2). Isaiah 26 is almost like one of the Songs of Ascent (Pss. 120—134) sung by pilgrims going up to Jerusalem for one of the annual festivals. This song reflects the spiritual journey of Israel to true faith in the Lord and final salvation through Him.

KINGDOM EXTRA

"In that day this song will be sung" (Is. 26:1). Isaiah is speaking futuristically about the restoration of Israel as well as "the day of the Lord." The "day of the Lord" holds great portent for every believer in Christ. As ones who have experienced the entry of [God's] kingdom in part, we are the ones who then can sing this song. The passage goes on to talk about the walls of salvation and open gates (of praise, see 60:18). The song of the Lord is a song of praise based on the salvation He has provided. As ones who enjoy the fruits of salvation, let us enter into His presence through the open gates of praise.[2]

Contrast the two cities in Isaiah 26:1–6:

- The strong city (vv. 1–4)

- The lofty city (vv. 5, 6)

Why do you think peace and trust are major characteristics of residents of the city of God? (Is. 26:3, 4)

Describe the way of the righteous and the way of the wicked.

- The way of the righteous (Is. 26:7–9)

- The way of the wicked (Is. 26:10, 11)

What will believing Israel remember in the future when they reflect on the peace of the city of God? (Is. 26:12–15)

When Israel had tried to save herself in the past by her own efforts, it had been like trying to give birth after a false pregnancy (Is. 26:16–18). In your experience, what has been the greatest frustration of trying to handle big issues of life without the help of the Spirit of God?

The Old Testament doesn't say a lot about the resurrection of the dead. Two of its clearest statements are in this portion of Isaiah about the last days (Is. 25:7, 8; 26:9). What do these passages say about the future of those who have died?

FAITH ALIVE

What are you doing to develop the heavenly habit of cultivating perfect peace in the Lord?

What could you do to cultivate the heavenly practices of desiring the Lord in the night and seeking Him early?

What are past masters from which the Lord has delivered you? What are present masters from which you need deliverance? How should you talk to the Lord about these two groups?

Visions of the Kingdom:
The Restoration of God's People

The final portion of Isaiah's panorama of the last days deals with God's method of purifying the remnant of Israel who will be saved during the day of the Lord. It is a message of salvation and judgment, of salvation through judgment. The medicine that will "heal" God's chosen people is very bitter but very effective.

Where did Isaiah picture the various participants being when the inhabitants of the earth are punished? (Is. 26:20—27:1)

- God's people (26:20)

- The Lord (26:21)

- Leviathan (27:1)

   Bible Extra

Leviathan is the name of a creature of chaos in ancient mythology, which is used by Isaiah as a type of God's enemies who were incited by Satan (Rev. 12:9). It thus personified evil, which God will ultimately slay.[3]

In Isaiah 5:1–7, the prophet used imagery of an unfruitful vineyard to illustrate the spiritual needs of Judah. In chapter 27, Isaiah used the image of a fruitful vineyard to illustrate restored Israel in the last days. What does the prophet say about each of these topics through the vineyard figure of speech? (Is. 27:2–6)

- God's care for His people

- God's protection of His people

- God's response to penitence

- God's blessing through His people

📖 BIBLE EXTRA

"He shall cause to take root . . . and fill the face of the world with fruit" (27:6). The promise of restoration wipes away the earlier disappointment of an unfruitful vineyard (see 5:1–7). Now the Lord is planting anew, watering daily (v. 3), clearing briars (v. 4), and promising expansive fruitfulness (v. 6). The picture is that of the Messiah, the true Vine (John 15:1–8), extending His disciples as fruit-bearing branches to the world. The fruit is the Lord's doing, yet He asks participants to come and be willing to be planted. Believers who are pliable before the Spirit—yielded to His direction and dynamic, willing to be stretched and sent forth—will bear much fruit.[4]

God will have to judge Israel's sins before the nation will respond in faith in the last days. How will that judgment differ from the judgment on the rest of the nations? (Is. 27:7–9)

How will God's judgment on Israel (and Jerusalem) be like His judgment on any other nation? (Is. 27:10, 11)

What figures of speech did Isaiah use to portray God gathering the believing remnant of Israel from these two areas? What does each figure say about the restorative work of God?

• Inside the Promised Land (Is. 27:12)

• Outside the Promised Land (Is. 27:13)

 FAITH ALIVE

How is the Spirit of God cultivating and cleansing your life as through it were a vineyard of the Lord?

In what ways is the Spirit of God increasing the fruitfulness of your life so you can share that fruitfulness with the world?

1. *Hayford's Bible Handbook* (Nashville: Thomas Nelson, 1995), 177, "Surveying Isaiah," note on Is. 24:21.

2. Ibid., 177, "Surveying Isaiah," note on Is. 26:1-4.

3. *Spirit-Filled Life® Bible* (Nashville: Thomas Nelson, 1991), 994, note on Is. 27:1.

4. *Hayford's Bible Handbook*, 177.

Lesson 5/ What Do You Think of God?
Isaiah 28—33

It's easy to begin to treat God as though He were a major appliance—a refrigerator or a dishwasher—valuable and very important, but still a convenience. Major appliances make life easier and better. We want God to do that too. But if my refrigerator stops working, I unplug it, get rid of it, and buy a new one. When life isn't going like we want it, it's tempting to think God has failed to do His job for us. Temptation says, "Unplug Him, move Him out in the garage of life, and trust something else."

Israel and Judah were doing this during the lifetime and ministry of Isaiah the prophet. The Assyrian Empire had armies marching all over the Near East, and the little kingdoms of Palestine thought Isaiah's advice to trust the Lord alone for deliverance seemed naive. Statesmanship, military tactics, modern weapon systems, and an alliance of small states with Egypt as their head seemed so much more sophisticated.

What do you think about God when your life is falling apart, when sinning looks like the advantageous thing to do or at least a lot of fun, or when you're tired of doing the right thing without apparent results?

DOES HIS WORD CRAMP YOUR STYLE?

Israel and Judah were bound to the Lord by the covenant of the Mosaic Law. They had been gifted with the ministries of speaking and writing prophets to provide the Word of the Lord at crucial moments. Yet they often wearied of keeping the covenant or heeding the prophets. It was as though they thought God's Word was a fine thing in the abstract, but not very realistic in the day-to-day hassles of real life.

WORD WEALTH

Woe translates a Hebrew interjection that occurs almost exclusively in the prophetic books to lament the physical judgment or chastening of God on His people or the surrounding nations. Isaiah 28—33 is sometimes called the Book of Woes because **woe** highlights every chapter except 32 (Is. 28:1; 29:1, 15; 30:1; 31:1; 33:1).

Samaria, the capital of the Northern Kingdom of Israel, regarded herself as a garland of flowers perched on the top of the mountains of Ephraim. Little did Samaria realize what a storm of judgment was about to break on her (Is. 28:1–4). The Lord was the true garland crowning the remnant who would survive because they trusted Him (vv. 5, 6). Alcohol was destroying the wisdom and judgment of Israel's leaders to the point that God had to treat them like children as He tried to draw them away from destruction (Is. 28:7–10).

What are some of the things in life that blind us to the spirit of pride which always draws our eyes away from God?

How has God been patient with you by teaching you His ways "precept upon precept, line upon line, here a little, there a little" (Is. 28:10)?

KINGDOM EXTRA

In Isaiah 28:11, 12, God used Isaiah to tell Judah that He would teach them in a manner they did not like and that He would give them knowledge through the language of foreigners as a sign of their unbelief. Centuries later the apostle Paul expands the intent of this passage, referring to the gift of speaking in tongues in the church as a manifestation or sign to unbelievers (1 Cor. 14:21, 22). This sign could be in languages either known or unknown to human beings (compare 1 Cor. 14 with Acts 2:1–11; 10:45, 46).[1]

Isaiah identified Judah with idolatrous Israel by sarcastically suggesting that they would like to replace the covenant of life made with the Lord with a covenant of death made with the grave (Is. 28:14, 15). Then he reminded them that only God's Messiah was a cornerstone that could be the foundation for upright lives. Everything else would be swept away in the storm of judgment (vv.16–22).

What lies of the modern world do you sometimes find tempting as alternatives to the absolute truth of God's Holy Word?

Isaiah used agricultural images to teach that God's judgments are not all the same. They fit the nation needing correction, and they even fit the stage of that nation's life (Is. 28:23–29).

How have you found that God has tailored His chastening to fit you and your life situation?

Proud Ariel (Jerusalem) would be brought nearly to the dust by the Assyrians (Is. 29:1–4). However, the mighty Assyrians, who could taste victory like a man in a dream, would be destroyed by God before completing the conquest (vv. 5–8). In spite of this marvelous promise, no one in Jerusalem had the insight to comprehend the Word of the Lord (vv. 9–12). All Jerusalem boasted was an empty religion (v. 13). Because they would learn nothing from their deliverance from Assyria, they would be conquered by Babylon a century later (v. 14). The ultimate sin of the people of Jerusalem was thinking they were independent of their Maker and able to get away with anything they wanted to (vv. 15, 16).

How can you protect yourself from falling into a rut of going through the motions of worship and service at church and keep your heart close to God?

In what kinds of situations do you need to remind yourself that God always sees you and knows what you are doing?

Of what practical value to you is the truth that God is the potter and you are the clay?

In spite of all the turmoil that Israel and Judah brought on themselves because they tried to evade God's Word, the Lord promised them a glorious future when all would comprehend that Word (Is. 29:17, 18). In that day God's justice will elevate the humble and abase the proud (vv. 19–21). All the history of God's chosen people would culminate in a generation which loves and obeys the Holy One of Israel (vv. 22–24).

What injustices in your life and the lives of others do you look forward to seeing corrected in the future kingdom of God?

Do You Trust In Something Else?

Isaiah was dismayed that Judah did not seek the Spirit of God as the source of her advice and plans (Is. 30:1). They wanted to reverse, in a sense, the Exodus from Egypt and find security there (vv. 2, 3). He pictured the emissaries from Judah making their dangerous journey to Egypt with beasts loaded with gifts, only to find Egypt impotent against Assyria (vv. 4–7). The Lord commanded the prophet to indict Judah for turning aside from the Law, the prophets, and from the Holy One of Israel (vv. 8–11).

In our day, the Holy Spirit baptizes and fills all who will receive Him. The moment-by-moment experience of the Spirit's guidance is itself a witness that we are God's children and the bridge to ministry beyond natural abilities. Yet we must desire and obey the Spirit's promptings. In what kinds of situations are you tempted to trust in human wisdom or strength rather than the Holy Spirit of God?

At such times, in whom or in what are you tempted to trust instead of the Holy Spirit?

Give an example from your life of turning aside from God's Word and Spirit to follow worldly counsel and advice.

Give an example from your life of rejecting worldly counsel and advice to follow God's Word and Spirit.

The Lord predicted that Judah would end up like a bulging wall that collapsed from strain and a clay pitcher shattered on the floor (Is. 30:12–14). Because they rejected His peace in favor of military might, they would be routed until only a tiny remnant remained (vv. 15–17). But the Lord would wait to replant that remnant in the Promised Land (vv. 18, 19). Out of affliction they would reject idolatry and walk in God's way (vv. 20–22). God's blessings on restored Judah would be a foretaste of the blessings of the future kingdom of God (vv. 23–26).

Why do you think we sometimes have to experience collapse and brokenness in our lives before we return to the Lord and His ways?

Why do you think depending on worldly wisdom leaves us susceptible to panic? (Is. 30:11)

In your experience, what are some ways you have heard the Lord directing you, "This is the way, walk in it"?

What have you learned about the blessings of the future kingdom of God from the way the Lord blesses you now?

Assyria, God's instrument of judgment on the nations, would in time be judged by the Lord as though He were a fire, a flood, a sieve, and a bit in a horse's mouth (Is. 30:27, 28). God's righteous remnant would rejoice as though at a festival when the voice of God struck down Assyria and condemned the bloody empire to Tophet (vv. 29–33).

 BIBLE EXTRA

Tophet was an Old Testament name for part of the Valley of Hinnom, southeast of Jerusalem, where child sacrifices were offered during the lifetime of Isaiah to Chemosh, a Moabite god, and Molech, an Ammonite god (1 Kin. 11:7; 2 Kin. 23:10, 13). Isaiah used Tophet as a symbol of God's judgment against Assyria. By Jesus' time this valley was called Gehenna (see Mark 9:42–48 where Gehenna is translated three times as "hell").[2]

What ungodly oppressors—habits, thought patterns, secret sins—would you like to see destroyed from your life so you can depend more fully on the Lord?

Write a prayer to God asking Him to judge these "oppressors" in your life. (Consider asking your pastor or other spiritual leader to counsel you and pray with you about this).

BIBLE EXTRA

The Teacher *Par Excellence* (Is. 30:19–26). The Messianic Teacher would provide expert guidance to His people (v. 21). They would hear a voice *behind* them. The picture is that of a shepherd who follows his flock and calls out directions to them. The unseen voice would call the people to repentance and return to the straight and narrow path. The

tacit assumption here is that the people will stray and conse-
quently will need the continuing ministry of the Teacher.[3]

The Egyptian army was renowned for horses, which most
military powers did not possess. Judah preferred this impressive weapon system to the spiritual power of God (Is. 31:1).
The spiritual might of God could overwhelm the powers of
armies—even horses (vv. 2, 3). Judah and Jerusalem needed to
learn that no power stands against God's people when He
roars like a lion to guard them (vv. 4–7). The Assyrian army
would die without a sword lifted against it (vv. 8, 9).

Give an example of a time when you trusted the Lord to
deliver you from a desperate situation and He protected you as
though He were a lion.

WHAT EFFECT DOES GOD'S SPIRIT HAVE ON YOU?

The idea of judgment drops into the background in Isaiah
32. The word "woe" does not introduce it as it does the other
five chapters in this section of the book. Isaiah foresaw the
kingdom of the Messiah in which He and His officials will rule
justly to create a safe and stimulating realm (Is. 32:1–4). In
this kingdom no foolish or evil person will appear to be wise or
good. All ungodliness will be exposed as an aspect of justice
(vv. 5–8).

For the rule of God to be expressed in your life, what gifts
and attitudes need to be stimulated by God's Spirit?

For the rule of God to be active in your life, what schemes
and devices of the devil do you need the Spirit's help in escaping? (See 2 Cor. 10:3–6; Eph. 6:10–18)

Before Judah could experience the kingdom of God, it
had to endure the chastisement of Assyria. Isaiah warned the
complacent women of Judah that in about a year they would
mourn mightily for the sorrow that would come on them, the

fruitfulness of the land, and the urban life of Jerusalem (Is. 32:9–14). After this judgment Isaiah's vision leapt to the out-pouring of God's Holy Spirit inaugurating the blessings of God's kingdom (v. 15). The homes of God's people in His kingdom will be made secure by justice, righteousness, and peace (vv. 16–18). No matter how severe temporary chasten-ing may be, the ultimate blessing is secure (vv. 19, 20).

What has God torn down and removed from your life in order to pour out His Spirit on you to establish His reign?

How is the Spirit of God strengthening your life in jus-tice, righteousness, and peace to give you a greater sense of spiritual security?

WHAT WILL HE THINK OF YOU IN THE END?

The Assyrians had earned God's enmity by their injustices and treachery as conquerors of the nations of the fertile cres-cent (Is. 33:1). Isaiah interceded on behalf of the remnant of God's people who would survive judgment (vv. 2–4). He anticipated the future glories of the kingdom of God (vv. 5, 6) while acknowledging the current devastation of Palestine (vv. 7–9).

Imagine God assessing your life and planning His will for you. What might He have in mind in each of these areas?
• Means of chastening and purification

• Goals for your character and service

The Lord said that He was about to rise in judgment (Is. 33:10), and that Judah would be consumed in the flames (vv. 11, 12). The proper response was to acknowledge His power (v. 13). Sinners, however, would fear the fires of judgment, while the righteous would be protected (vv. 14–16).

How do you see the mighty power of God at work around you? How should you respond to God when you observe His power in these ways?

In the trials of daily life how do you observe the wicked failing and the righteous enduring?
• The wicked

• The righteous

Isaiah 33:17–24 begins to describe the recovery of Judah from the Assyrian invasion, but the language of the paragraph quickly points beyond ordinary events to the future kingdom of God. The coming King will rule a wide territory from a great capital free from threatening enemies (vv. 17–19). Jerusalem, that capital, will be a center of abiding peace, worship, beauty, prosperity, and health (vv. 20–24).

How has the reign of Christ brought beauty (Is. 33:17) into your life in each of these areas that will characterize the New Jerusalem?
• Tranquility

• Reverence

• Fruitfulness

• Health of body or spirit

1. *Spirit-Filled Life® Bible* (Nashville: Thomas Nelson, 1991), 2019, "Holy Spirit Gifts and Power."

2. *Nelson's New Illustrated Bible Dictionary* (Nashville: Thomas Nelson, 1995), 1269, "Tophet."

3. James Smith, *What the Bible Teaches about the Promised Messiah* (Nashville: Thomas Nelson, 1993), 280.

Lesson 6/Trash or Treasure?
Isaiah 34—35

Pierre Auguste Renoir pioneered impressionist techniques in French painting late in the nineteenth century. As the fame of Renoir spread, so did the number of Renoir forgeries. The painter was understandably upset by the proliferation of these bogus pictures, mere trash alongside the treasures of his artistry, but after a time he came to accept their presence.

As a favor to collectors he liked who had been stuck with one of these fakes, Renoir occasionally touched up a canvas and signed it so that the collector could display or resell it as an original. Angry friends urged him to take legal action against the forgers, but Renoir could see no benefit in the litigation. He pointed out, "It takes less time to touch up a painting than to go to court about it."[1]

Like Renoir, the Lord has no desire to bring judgment on mankind. He prefers to rescue the ruined canvases of sinful lives. Eventually, however, the unredeemed forgeries must be exposed and destroyed so that the real people of God can shine in all His glory.

TAKING OUT THE TRASH—JUDGMENT SUMMARY

Isaiah 34—35 takes the ideas of judgment and blessing developed in chapters 28—33, extends them into the future, and uses them to describe the day of the Lord. Isaiah 34 treats the judgment theme. Edom, a little nation located southeast of the Dead Sea with a special relationship to Israel, is used to represent all the evil nations of the earth. On the day of the Lord, God will be in a spring cleaning mood, and Edom represents all the trash accumulated through the long winter of human history.

To begin chapter 34, Isaiah announced a climactic expression of the Lord's judgment on evil. Summarize this judgment according to these components.

- Those it concerns (Is. 34:1, 2)

- The Lord's motivation (Is. 34:2)

- Its dreadfulness (Is. 34:3)

- Its "last days" character (Is. 34:4)

 BIBLE EXTRA

"'Was not Esau Jacob's brother,' says the Lord. 'Yet Jacob I have loved, but Esau I have hated'" (Mal. 1:2, 3). Esau and Jacob were in fact twin brothers, and Esau was the older of the two. Esau had every right to expect to be blessed by their father Isaac as the heir of the promise of God to Abraham. But the younger son was blessed, and his offspring named Israel; the older son was left to stew over his loss, and his descendants were called Edom.

"The very fact that Jacob was chosen, 'loved,' meant that Esau was rejected, 'hated,' rejection being implicit in the exercise of choice. Personal animosity toward Esau is not implied. Esau and his descendants, however, by nursing resentment and showing hostility toward Jacob, did bring God's judgment on themselves."[2] Isaiah contrasted Edom and Israel in chapters 34 and 35 as representatives of the world and the people of God.

Although the Lord's sword will be turned against the heavens, its real object will be judgment on the unbelieving nations (Is. 34:5). To what does the Lord compare His slaughter of the unbelieving nations (represented by Edom)? (Is. 34:6–7)

How does this gory comparison with sacrifice give greater meaning to the battle resulting in such butchery? (Is. 34:6, 7)

WORD WEALTH

Utterly destroyed (Is. 34:2) translates a Hebrew verb and **curse** (v. 5) translates a noun from the same Hebrew word family. They have the same consonants but different vowels. The most familiar biblical use of this word group occurs in Joshua when the city of Jericho was called "accursed" (Josh. 7:11, "devoted," KJV). The accursed things belonged exclusively to the Lord. Arabic has the same words in its vocabulary, and the noun entered English after the Crusades. It is "harem" and indicated that which belonged solely to the sheik or emperor. God claims the unbelieving nations are His, and His alone, to judge.

Why will the Lord judge the nations in the last days? (Is. 34:8)

How will His judgment on the unbelieving nations be similar to His destruction of Sodom and Gomorrah? (Is. 34:9, 10; see Gen. 19:24–28)

Edom, the descendants of Jacob's brother Esau, had carved a prosperous existence out of desert land. How did Isaiah describe the earth after the Lord will judge the unbelieving nations in the last days? (Is. 34:11–15)

In Isaiah 28:16, 17, the prophet used imagery of a building stone and a measuring line to speak of God constructing His people's future. In Isaiah 34:11b the prophet uses measuring line and building stone imagery about "constructing" des-

olation. Read the two passages and compare the meaning of
the architectural figures of speech.

- Isaiah 28:16, 17

- Isaiah 34:11b

Judgment is an unappealing topic, but it is a major theme
of the book of Isaiah [called "the book of the Lord" (34:16)].
The Spirit of the Lord will superintend the desolating of the
earth in judgment, even as He hovered over the waters as the
earth was first formed (Gen. 1:2). What do you think are some
of the lessons we as believers in Jesus Christ should learn from
the pervasive biblical message that unbelievers will suffer judgment and eternal punishment?

Sprucing Up the Treasure—Blessing Summary

The poetry of the first section of the book of Isaiah
reaches its pinnacle in chapter 35. Not until chapter 40 will the
language of Isaiah sing so beautifully. This is not an accident.
Chapters 36—39 make a transition from the part of Isaiah set
against the backdrop of God's judgment through Assyria to
the part set against the backdrop of His judgment through
Babylon. It is fitting that the poetic style of chapter 35 should
rise to touch the mood and themes of chapter 40. Spring
cleaning is over. The trash has been hauled away, and the sum-
mer of God's blessing on the treasure His people bursts into
blossom.

In what ways is Isaiah 35:1, 2 the reverse of 34:8–15?

The wilderness in view in Isaiah 35:1 appears to be the
one across which a highway will be built (v. 8) for use of which
travelers will need strength (v. 3). Isaiah was glimpsing the
return of Judah from Babylon more than 200 years in the

future, and he was seeing even further to the day of the Lord when believing Jews will flock to the Messiah's millennial reign based in Jerusalem.

How did Isaiah summarize what will happen to the desolate areas when the people of God are gathered to Jerusalem in the last days? (Is. 35:1, 2)

How will the Lord prepare those who are not ready to travel (Is. 35:3) according to each of these passages?
• Isaiah 35:4 (see 34:8)

• Isaiah 35:5, 6a

• Isaiah 35:6b, 7

 BIBLE EXTRA

Look up Luke 7:18–23 and write out the phrases you find in those verses that correspond to expressions in Isaiah 35:3–6.

What does Jesus want John the Baptist to conclude from His quoting this part of Isaiah?

Read this excerpt from *Hayford's Bible Handbook.*

The "good news of the kingdom" (Matt. 3:2; 4:17; 10:7; Luke 10:9) . . . announces that this righteous, saving, and restoring rule of God is present through the words and deeds of Jesus, including the ministry to which Jesus commissions His followers. The core concept of the "kingdom of God" is God's saving *action* and the new life His acts bring to believers. . . . Jesus not only teaches about the kingdom of God, but He also actuates God's saving reign when He heals the blind, lame, deaf, and leprous; when He casts out demons; when He raises the dead; when He expresses God's tender affection for the underclass and outcasts. In Jesus, that crucial part of the "day of the Lord" known as the "day of salvation" has arrived.

Based on this excerpt and what you have studied so far in Isaiah, describe the extent to which the kingdom of God, the saving reign of God, has arrived through the ministry of Jesus, as well as the extent to which the kingdom is still future.

KINGDOM EXTRA

"Behold your God will come with vengeance, with the recompense of God" (Is. 35:4). The coming of the Lord will be purposeful, bringing to an end the destructive works of darkness and meting out His justice in the interest of His children. One of the clear indicators of the certainty and imminence of His return is the presence of the kinds of things described in verses 5 and 6: when the kingdom is ministered with power and understanding, and blind eyes and deaf ears begin to be opened, we can enthusiastically declare the Second Coming of Jesus.[3]

The Hebrew term for "highway" has the same sense as the English word—a road built up higher than the terrain it passes through (Is. 35:8). How is the road the Lord provides back to Jerusalem both metaphorically and literally a highway?

• Metaphorically (Is. 35:8)

• Literally (Is. 35:9)

Who are the treasures God will take such great care of?
(Is. 35:10a)

What will these treasured people experience when they
reach Jerusalem and the Messiah's reign? (Is. 35:10)

 FAITH ALIVE

Believers in Jesus Christ are God's treasured posses-
sions today (Eph. 1:14; 1 Pet. 2:9). How has God prepared a
way before you through the circumstances of your life?

How has He strengthened you to cope with the difficulties of life?

How has He brought joy and gladness into your heart?

THE HOLY ONE OF ISRAEL SAVES—ISAIAH 1—35 SUMMARY

Isaiah clearly proclaimed that our God is an awesome
God. We don't care to think about judgment much, but the
first thirty-five chapters of the book of Isaiah deal mainly with
judgment: of Judah and Jerusalem (Is. 1—12), of the nations
(13—27), and of Israel and Judah as the sum of God's people
(28—35). All three of these sections are interspersed with
promises of God's blessing on those who believe. The connection between judgment and blessing is that God takes out the
trash in order to display His treasures.

It's impossible to understand God's work in judgment
and blessing without understanding His awesome character.

Look up the following passages from the first half of Isaiah and record what they have to say about the Holy One of Israel.

- Isaiah 1:10–20

- Isaiah 6:1–13

- Isaiah 8:12–15

- Isaiah 9:1–7

- Isaiah 10:20–23

- Isaiah 12:1–6

- Isaiah 24:1–3, 19–23

- Isaiah 25:1–9

- Isaiah 28:5, 6

- Isaiah 33:22

What do you learn about the Messiah from each of these passages in the first part of Isaiah?

- Isaiah 7:14

- Isaiah 9:6, 7

- Isaiah 11:1–5

Look up the verses in the chart below that capture the historical and futuristic essence of each segment of the first thirty-five chapters of Isaiah and write a summary for each in the space provided. For each segment dealing with the future, tell the extent to which those prophecies are fulfilled in the earthly ministry of Jesus and through His church.

Our God Is an Awesome God

(1)   Awesome in Judah and Jerusalem   Then (Is. 3:1–12)
(10) -- (11) Future (Is. 11:1–10)
(12)
(13)   Awesome among the Nations of the World   Then (Is. 17:12–14)
(23) -- (24) Future (Is. 25:6–9; 26:1–6)
(27)

(28)   Awesome in Israel and Judah
    Then (Is. 32:9–15)

(33)
----
(34) Future (Is. 35:3–10)

(35)

    FAITH ALIVE

How can the truths of Isaiah 1—35 enrich your praise and worship of God, the Holy One of Israel?

What has Isaiah 1—35 taught you about what God expects of you in terms of justice and righteousness?

What have you learned about the saving reign of God in the present and the future of the godly and the ungodly?

1. James S. Hewett, ed., *Illustrations Unlimited* (Wheaton, IL: Tyndale House Publishers, 1988), 489.

2. Joyce G. Baldwin. *Haggai, Zechariah, Malachi: An Introduction and Commentary* (Downers Grove, IL: InterVarsity Press, 1972), 222–223.

3. *Hayford's Bible Handbook* (Nashville: Thomas Nelson , 1995), 178.

Lesson 7/Out of the Frying Pan into the Fire
Isaiah 36—39

Farmer Brown had three sons—Jim, John, and Sam—all hard-drinking, rowdy fellows who never darkened the door of the little frame church up the creek. One day a rattlesnake bit Sam, and the doctor was away. The preacher was visiting a neighbor, so when Sam's leg was swelled up real good, Jim saddled his horse and fetched him.

Preacher Jones looked around the bedroom at old man Brown and Jim and John, who looked downright subdued. Sam lay on the feather bed, feverish and swollen. "You got to pray for me, Preacher Jones," he croaked.

The preacher took off his hat and began to pray. "Almighty God, thank Thee for sending this rattlesnake to bite Sam. He ain't never been inside the church house and he ain't never prayed or thought about Thee. Teach him a lesson, Lord, and make him repent.

"And now, O Father, send another rattlesnake to bite Jim, and another to bite John, and a really big one to bite their old man. For years we done everything we knowed to get them to turn to Thee, but nothing worked. This rattlesnake has done more good than I ever did. So I reckon the onliest thing for this family is more rattlesnakes. So Lord, send us bigger and meaner rattlesnakes. Amen."[1]

THE BIGGER THEY ARE . . .

The army of the Assyrian Empire was like that rattlesnake that bit Sam Brown. It had conquered and deported the hopelessly idolatrous Northern Kingdom of Israel and gotten the attention of many people in Judah. The invaders from Nineveh were certainly the mightiest military power ever to march through Palestine.

How did the Assyrian emperor Sennacherib prepare before launching an attack on Jerusalem? (Is. 36:1)

Assyrian Campaign Against Judah (701 B.C.). Sennacherib moved southward along the coastal plains to Lachish and camped against Jerusalem in 701 B.C.[2]

Sennacherib sent an envoy whose title was the Rabshakah to try and negotiate the surrender of Jerusalem and Judah to him (Is. 36:2). King Hezekiah in turn appointed three officials to meet with the Assyrian ambassador (v. 3). How did the Rabshakah refer to the king of Judah and the emperor of Assyria (Is. 36:4)? What was he implying by these different forms of address?

WORD WEALTH

Rabshakah literally meant chief cupbearer in Aramaic, the diplomatic language of the ancient Near East. Cupbearers had to be men whom emperors trusted with their lives since they guarded him from being poisoned. The title tended to become honorary and indicate a confidential official. In the Assyrian Empire, Rabshakah was a military title, such as field commander[3] or chief of staff.[4]

The message from the invading Assyrians proposed eight reasons why the Judeans should surrender without a fight. What were they?

1. (Is. 36:5)

2. (Is. 36:6)

3. (Is. 36:7)

4. (Is. 36:8, 9)

5. (Is. 36:10)

6. (Is. 36:14, 15, 18)

7. (Is. 36:16, 17)

8. (Is. 36:18–20)

Why did the representatives from Hezekiah's court want the Rabshakah to present the Assyrian message in Aramaic rather than Hebrew? (Is. 36:11, 12)

Why did the Rabshakah only speak louder in Hebrew rather than switching to Aramaic?

What were the various responses to the Rabshakah's message and what did the responses indicate about Judah's attitude toward its situation?
- The people on the wall who heard the Rabshakah (Is. 36:21)

- Eliakim, Shebna, and Joah (Is. 36:22)

FAITH ALIVE

What forces in the world do you find intimidating?

What approaches does the devil take to you to convince you that you should fear these forces of the world?

How do you tend to respond when these forces of the world intimidate you?

. . . THE HARDER THEY FALL

King Hezekiah responded especially well to the threat of the Assyrians. He didn't need to be bitten by the rattlesnake before he called for the prayers of the man of God.

How did King Hezekiah respond to the ultimatum delivered by the Rabshakah from Sennacherib? (Is. 37:1–4)

What did the Lord say to Hezekiah through Isaiah about the following?
- Hezekiah's response to Sennacherib (Is. 37:6)

- The fate of Sennacherib (Is. 37:7)

What was Assyria's first hint that it was in trouble trying to capture Jerusalem? (Is. 37:8, 9)

How did Sennacherib try to intimidate Hezekiah while he left to deal with the Ethiopian army? (Is. 37:9b–13)

Analyze Hezekiah's prayer according to the following topics.
- Approach to the Lord (Is. 37:14)

- Invocation (Is. 37:16)

- Appeal (Is. 37:17)

- Acknowledgment (Is. 37:18, 19)

- Petition (Is. 37:20)

KINGDOM EXTRA

Sennacherib's threat to destroy Hezekiah reminds us that the righteous are often overtaken by trouble. If Sennacherib had taken Jerusalem, the Jews could have ceased to exist as a nation. The messianic promise of God's kingdom's eventually triumphing on Earth was in the balance. But when Hezekiah and Isaiah prayed, God intervened with a demonstration of supernatural power that proved to Assyria that He was God indeed (37:36).[5]

Summarize the various parts of Isaiah's prediction about Sennacherib and Assyria that came in answer to Hezekiah's prayer (Is. 37:22–35).

- Judah's attitude (v. 22)

- Assyria's blasphemy (vv. 23–25)

- God's sovereign control (vv. 26, 27)

- Assyria's destiny (vv. 28, 29)

- Judah's recovery from invasion (vv. 30–32)

- Assyria at Jerusalem (vv. 33–35)

How was the prophecy of Isaiah about Assyria and Sennacherib fulfilled? (Is. 37:36–38)

FAITH ALIVE

How can you lay out your troubles before the Lord as clearly as Hezekiah did when he took Sennacherib's letter into the temple and spread it out before the Lord?

What do you learn from Hezekiah's prayer about how you should pray about difficulties you are facing?

WINNING THE BATTLE . . .

Assyria may have been a nasty rattlesnake, but the spiritual problems of Judah and Jerusalem were going to require the intervention of a bigger, meaner rattlesnake, namely Babylon. Isaiah 38 and 39 hint at the spiritual issues that would emerge in Judah after God's miraculous delivery of His people from Assyria. These chapters laid the groundwork for the focus on Babylon in chapters 40—66. Isaiah 38:6 places the events of chapters 38 and 39 chronologically before chapters 36 and 37. They are placed later because they explain how Babylon got interested in Judah as a land to conquer.

Describe the main sequence of events surrounding Hezekiah's health.

1. Hezekiah's problem (Is. 38:1a, 21)

2. Isaiah's first prediction (Is. 38:1b)

3. Hezekiah's response (Is. 38:2, 3)

4. Isaiah's second prediction (Is. 38:4–6)

5. Hezekiah's treatment (Is. 38:21)

6. Hezekiah's demand (Is. 38:22)

7. The Lord's response (Is. 38:7, 8)

After Hezekiah miraculously recovered, he wrote a psalm that recorded his thoughts about impending death (Is. 38:10–14) and his thoughts about God's gracious restoration of his health (vv. 15–20). Summarize his prayer about these matters.

• Reasons Hezekiah wanted to live (Is. 38:10, 11)

• How Hezekiah responded to imminent death (Is. 38:12–14)

• Hezekiah's thoughts about personal peace (Is. 38:13–17)

• Hezekiah's thoughts about praise (Is. 38:18–20)

 FAITH ALIVE

The fifteen years the Lord added to Hezekiah's life were very important. His heir was born in that time; Manasseh was only twelve years old when Hezekiah died (2 Kin. 21:1). The magnificent stand of Hezekiah against Sennacherib (Is. 36—

37) probably happened shortly after the healing. But Hezekiah sometimes had trouble recognizing that God the Healer and Giver was of more significance than the healing and the gift. In Isaiah 39, Hezekiah acted rashly because he was excited about and proud of his newly restored health. What are the greatest gifts the Lord has given you?

How can you keep your eyes on knowing the Giver more than on possessing the gifts?

. . . But Losing the War

While King Hezekiah was flushed with enthusiasm for his newly extended life and excited about his future, he inadvertently invited the worst rattlesnake around into his house. At the time Babylon was subject to Assyria. It was a baby rattlesnake, but it had a long family history of venomous activity.

Why do you think Hezekiah was so pleased and flattered that the ruler of Babylon sent envoys with a message congratulating him on recovering his health? (Is. 39:1, 2a)

Why do you think Hezekiah entertained his Babylonian guests by showing them all the treasures accumulated through the centuries of the Davidic dynasty? (Is. 39:2)

Hezekiah had not consulted with Isaiah about how God wanted him to deal with the Babylonian ambassadors. After reading Isaiah's questions and Hezekiah's answers to them, circle the numbers on the scales that show how you rate each man's concern about what had happened. (Is. 39:3, 4)

Isaiah's Concern

1	2	3	4	5	6	7	8	9	10
Every-thing Is Great			Things Seem Okay			Something Is Fishy			Things Are Terrible

Hezekiah's Concern

1	2	3	4	5	6	7	8	9	10
Every-thing Is Great			Things Seem Okay			Something Is Fishy			Things Are Terrible

What was the message of the Lord of Hosts to Hezekiah concerning the results of his adventure with the Babylonian representatives? (Is. 39:5–7)

What was Hezekiah's response to this prophecy of Isaiah (Is. 39:8)

Do you think Hezekiah's response reveals mature acceptance of his responsibility or immature relief at escaping the consequences of his rashness (Is. 39:8)? Why do you think so?

FAITH ALIVE

It was more than 100 years before the Babylonians conquered Judah in fulfillment of Isaiah 39:6, 7. The other rattlesnake was still a ways off. Hezekiah had thought it good to have the stamp of Babylon's approval on God's work of healing. He was wrong.

What spiritual risks do we take when we look for the approval of unbelievers concerning our lives and ministries?

How do you think the Spirit of God warns us when we are getting too cozy with the world?

1. James S. Hewett, ed., *Illustrations Unlimited* (Wheaton, IL: Tyndale House Publishers, 1988), 187–188.

2. *Spirit-Filled Life® Bible* (Nashville: Thomas Nelson, 1991), 556, map of Assyrian Campaign Against Judah.

3. G. W. Grogan, "Isaiah," *The Expositor's Bible Commentary*, Vol. 6 (Grand Rapids, MI: Zondervan Publishing House, 1986), 227.

4. *Spirit-Filled Life® Bible*, 1007, note on Is. 36:2.

5. Ibid., 1007, "Kingdom Dynamics: Is. 36:1—37:38, God Intervenes with Power."

Part II:
Our God Is a Healing God:
Longing for the Saving Reign
of God
Isaiah 40—66

At chapter 40 the prophet Isaiah broke into the most exquisite poetry the Hebrew language has produced. He winged into the future to sing the praises of the living God who will give you eagles' wings to rise above the weary world that would wear you down with its cares.

Isaiah urged his readers to shape their behavior around the holiness of God and to base their hopes on the comfort God will give those who depend on Him. The LORD is the living God, Isaiah proclaimed. All other deities are human creations. The Holy One of Israel is the only One who can heal the hearts and lives of those who put their faith in Him.

Lesson 8/One Live God and Lots of Dead Ones
Isaiah 40:1—44:23

As the first millennium ended, Europe was gripped with a certainty that the living God would not allow the land of Jesus to belong to Islam. The First Crusade seemed to bear out Christian confidence. Urban II called for an army of liberation, and French counts and dukes responded with their personal armies. By 1099 Jerusalem was taken and Godfrey of Bouillon declared king. Europe rejoiced that the star and crescent of Allah had fallen before the cross of Christ.

Fifty years later Eugenius III called for a second crusade when Islamic forces threatened to retake the Holy City. German and French armies set out for Palestine along the same route as before, but they lost almost every engagement in Asia Minor, Syria, and Lebanon. They never reached Jerusalem, and Saladin conquered it after a symbolic siege in 1187.

Europe would never be the same again. In popular thinking Allah had defeated Christ. Either Allah was the living god, or neither he nor Christ was and the better army had won. Bernard of Clairvaux suggested that the ways of God often escape human understanding and wondered aloud if the defeat might not be punishment for Christian sins.[1] No one wanted to hear that.

THE UNAPPROACHABLE GOD APPROACHES

God had shown Isaiah that His people Judah would be defeated by the Babylonians as punishment for centuries of faithless idolatry. He also showed the prophet a time of future restoration and glory for a purified remnant. Judah would know God by watching Him keep His Word.

How did Isaiah preview the message of chapters 40—66? (Is. 40:1, 2)

Isaiah foresaw a forerunner of the day of the Lord. In part John the Baptist fulfilled this mission (Luke 3:4–6). Part of the prophecy still refers to a future time. What does the voice in the wilderness say about the glory of God and the glory of humanity?

• The glory of God (Is. 40:3–5)

• The glory of humanity (Is. 40:6–8)

BIBLE EXTRA

Look up Matthew 3:3 (with parallels Mark 1:3, Luke 3:4–6, John 1:23). According to these verses, what did the Gospel writers believe was the fulfillment of Isaiah 40:3–5?

Use a Bible concordance and look up as many New Testament references to "glory" as you can in ten minutes. List below all those references in which "glory" refers clearly to Jesus Christ the person or to His works.

In what ways is Christ, the glory of God, revealed and shining forth in the world today?

From what you know about Bible prophecy concerning the Second Coming of Christ, in what ways will His yet-future revelation manifest the glory of God more fully?

What are the good tidings Jerusalem will proclaim in the future? (Is. 40:9–11)

 BIBLE EXTRA

This picture of the Messiah as a shepherd invokes other key Bible passages comparing God's care for His people with a shepherd's care for a flock. Look up the following verses and note briefly what the image of a shepherd communicates about God and His Messiah, Jesus:

Psalm 80:1

Ezekiel 34:23

Micah 5:4

John 10:1–18

How did Isaiah contrast the living God with the nations of the earth? (Is. 40:12–17)

What is wrong with the creative processes idolators go through to conceive their gods? (Is. 40:18–20)

What is the living God like who promises to come near and comfort His people? (Is. 40:21–26)

What conclusions can we draw based on Isaiah 40?
- About God (Is. 40:27, 28)

- About those who trust Him (Is. 40:29–31)

FAITH ALIVE

In what circumstances of your life has God shown Himself to you as the awesome God who is greater than anyone can begin to imagine?

In what circumstances of your life has God shown Himself to you as the healing God who cares for you like a gentle Shepherd?

GOD VERSUS THE IDOLS

God called all of the ancient nations into His courtroom (Is. 41:1). For the first time, Isaiah's prophecy leaped ahead and looked back on the defeat of Babylon by Persia under the leadership of Cyrus (v. 2). Through the rest of Isaiah, Cyrus is viewed as an unwitting servant of the Lord to restore Judah to the Promised Land. How did Isaiah describe Cyrus the Persian's mission? (Is. 41:2–4)

How would the nations react to the sweeping conquests of Cyrus, whom God would raise up? (Is. 41:5–7)

How did the Lord counsel His people to respond to the Persian conqueror? (Is. 41:8–10)

WORD WEALTH

Servant (Is. 41:8) is a crucial term in Isaiah 40—66. Like many concepts in Isaiah **servant** has layers of meaning that become increasingly obvious as the prophecy unfolds. Basically, a **servant** is someone committed to advancing the purposes of God's kingdom on the earth. Israel was God's servant, but not a faithful one (41:8-10). Out of Isaiah's description of Israel as God's national servant emerges an individual who embodies all that Israel was meant to be (49:3–6). This Servant is the Messiah (52:13—53:12).

What did the Lord promise would eventually happen in the relations between the mighty nations and puny Israel? (Is. 41:11–16)

What does God promise to do for the helpless among those who depend on Him? (Is. 41:17–20)

What was the first challenge the Holy One of Israel issued to the idols and what was its result? (Is. 41:21–24)

How did the idols do in delivering the nations (including Judah when she trusted them) from the conquerors the living God sent among them? (Is. 41:25–29)

FAITH ALIVE

Why do you think we are tempted to give our allegiance to things around us that are ultimately of our own devising rather than to the living God?

What can we do to keep our spiritual focus on the Holy One of Israel instead of worldly sources of security and power?

THE SPIRIT-ANOINTED SERVANT OF THE LORD

In 1892 Bernhard Duhm published a German commentary *Das Buch Jesaia* in which he called four passages in Isaiah the Servant Songs. The label has stuck to Isaiah 42:1–4; 49:1–6; 50:4–9; and 52:13—53:12. In this first Servant Song, the Lord established the essential connection between the messianic Servant and the Holy Spirit.

How did the Lord describe His Servant and the servant's mission? (Is. 42:1–4)

📖 BIBLE EXTRA

Isaiah 40:1–4 is taken up in key passages in the Gospels. Look up the following references, and write down the phrases that come from this passage in Isaiah. Then tell what the portions from Isaiah seem to mean as they are used in the Gospels.

Matthew 12:9–21

Luke 3:21–22

Luke 4:1, 14–21

What did the Lord have to say when commissioning His Servant? (Is. 42:5–9)

What response to the news of the Servant's mission did Isaiah request from the farthest gentile nations (the coastlands) and the nearby tribes of Arabia (Kedar) and Edom (Sela)? (Is. 42:10–13)

KINGDOM EXTRA

"Sing to the Lord a new song" (Is. 42:10–12). This prophetic exhortation reflects the many times David included this activity in his own devotional walk. The value of singing new songs (that is, songs in the Spirit or in your spoken language that are not of previous composition) has tremendous devotional impact for the believer. "New songs" born of the Spirit of God can help break through spiritual barriers when nothing else seems to be working.[2]

In the second half of Isaiah 42, the Lord called Israel "My servant." This servant's humility springs from a different source than the Messiah's described in verses 2 through 4. What judgment awaited God's people because of their idolatry? (Is. 42:14–20)

What role did the Word of God play in the judgment facing God's people in Isaiah's day? (Is. 42:21–25)

FAITH ALIVE

Both you and the Lord Jesus can be called servants of the Lord. How is your role as a servant similar to and different from Christ's role as the Servant?
• Similar

• Different

What does it mean to you that the Spirit of God causes Christ to treat us gently and justly? (Is. 42:1–4)

THE REDEEMER OF ISRAEL AND HIS COUNTERFEITS

The final two chapters of this portion of Isaiah rejoice in the salvation Israel had been given and the Savior who loved them. This section ends with the longest and most detailed of the passages that mock idolatry. The false saviors are seen in the truest light when compared with the Holy One of Israel.

Why did the Lord insist Israel had no reason to fear in the present? (Is. 43:1–4)

Why did the Lord say Israel's descendants had no reason to fear in the future? (Is. 43:5–7)

What could Israel—even spiritually blind and deaf Israel—testify about the Lord to the nations? (Is. 43:8–13)

What would Israel—spiritually restored Israel—be able in the future to testify concerning the Lord to the nations? (Is. 43:14–21)

  WORD WEALTH

Redeemer (Is. 43:14; 44:6) translates the Hebrew noun that figures so prominently in the book of Ruth as the kinsman redeemer. Whenever God calls Himself Israel's Redeemer, He is declaring that He stands in close relationship to them. A kinsman redeemer was supposed to deliver his near kinsman from debt, from slavery, or from any other calamity that left him helpless. The Lord, who obligated Himself to Abraham and his descendants by covenant, redeemed Israel from Egypt by means of the Passover sacrifice and His mighty deeds. After the Babylonian captivity, He would redeem Israel again through the unwitting service of Cyrus the Persian emperor.

How did the Lord, who stands ready to blot out His people's sins, evaluate the spiritual condition of Judah that necessitated the Babylonian captivity? (Is. 43:22–28)

After stating categorically that Judah's sins would lead to judgment, the Lord called the nation His servant once more (Is. 44:1) and for the third time in this section urged the people not to fear (v. 2). What future blessings would the Spirit of God bring to His people? (Is. 44:3–5)

 KINGDOM EXTRA

"I will pour My Spirit on your descendants" (Is. 44:3). The vivid picture of a flood saturating dry, parched ground portrays the expansive and satisfying dimension of the Spirit's blessing. The simple qualification for reception is *desire*—recognizing our need for refreshing, and responding by earnestly seeking His presence. As the Spirit's refreshment is seen in and through us, others are drawn to the fountain of His living water.[3]

List the names of God found in Isaiah 44:6–8 and briefly express what each means to you.

1.

2.

3.

4.

5.

6.

The living God arranges the course of history and He can prepare His people for it in advance (Is. 44:7, 8). The idols are powerless. They ordain nothing; they foretell nothing; they redeem no one. How did the idolators bear witness against themselves? (Is. 44:9–12)

What are the fallacies in the story of making an idol in Isaiah 44:13–20?
- Logical fallacies

- Spiritual fallacies

FAITH ALIVE

Isaiah 44:21–23 contains a short psalm in which the Lord reminded Israel that He was their Redeemer and in which Isaiah invited the heavens and earth to praise Him for that redemption.

Write yourself a reminder of all God has done for you as your Redeemer. Write it as Isaiah did from God's point of view ("Remember what I have done for you").

Write a response of praise to God your Redeemer. Feel free to call on anyone or anything else to join you in praising the Lord.

1. Will Durant, *The Age of Faith* (New York: Simon and Schuster, 1950), 595.

2. *Hayford's Bible Handbook* (Nashville: Thomas Nelson, 1995), 179, "Surveying Isaiah, note on Is. 42:10–12."

3. Ibid., 180, "Surveying Isaiah, note on Is. 44:3."

Lesson 9/ Nothing Is Too Hard for God
Isaiah 44:24—48:22

The young G.I. was tasting World War II combat for the first time in a bloody battle in the Italian mountains. He dived into a foxhole just ahead of some bullets and began deepening the shallow pit. As he frantically scraped with his hands, he unearthed something metal. It was a silver crucifix, lost by a former foxhole occupant.

Another man hurtled in beside the frightened soldier as a new round of artillery screamed overhead. After the explosions, the soldier noticed his companion was a chaplain. Holding out the crucifix, the soldier gasped, "Am I glad to see you! How do you work this thing?"[1]

It seems we always want to be able to manipulate the power of God to our advantage. We try to use prayer to talk God into seeing things our way. We offer God bargains— church attendance and tithing in exchange for business success or children who don't go nuts when they're teenagers.

But God has plans of His own, and He expects us to fall in line behind Him to have the adventure of a lifetime. There is nothing too hard for God. He makes big plans and He wants people of big faith to carry them out.

HE MOLDS HISTORY LIKE CLAY

God has made the raw materials of history: the heavens and the earth, people and nations, even time. He is the Potter; we are the clay, both as individuals and entire civilizations. The immediate proof God offered of this through the prophet Isaiah was a series of predictions about Cyrus the Persian emperor. Isaiah named Cyrus more than 150 years before Persia amounted to anything.

List the activities found in Isaiah 44:24–28 that the Lord asserts that He engages in as the sovereign Master of world events.

Isaiah 24:1–3a describes the complete domination the Lord gave to Cyrus over the nations of the ancient Near East. Why did God bless Cyrus so? (Is. 45:3b, 4)

What evidence does the Lord offer that there is no other god beside Him? (Is. 45:5–8)

What woes do you think await people who deny or resist the activity of God as the Potter or the Originator of their lives? (Is. 45:9, 10)

What did God want His people asking Him about during the ministry of Isaiah? (Is. 45:11–13)

    KINGDOM EXTRA

"Ask Me of things to come" (Is. 45:11). In the Gospel of John (16:13) Jesus discusses the coming of the Holy Spirit of promise. He assures us that we, kingdom people, can expect to hear from the Lord. In fact, God speaks to us far more than we tend to listen! The issue is not whether God speaks to us but whether we are hearing Him.[2]

What did the Lord want the nations to learn from each of the following to prove that He alone is God?

- Cyrus' conquest (Is. 45:14)

- Israel's restoration (Is. 45:15–17)

- God's Word in creation and Scripture (Is. 45:18, 19)

- The impotence of their idols (Is. 45:20, 21)

- His offer of glorious salvation (Is. 45:22–25)

 KINGDOM EXTRA

"Look to Me and be saved, all you ends of the earth!" (Is. 45:22, 23). God extends His revelation to those who seek Him (v. 19), even to the idolator who has strayed from truth (v. 20). God consistently extends the invitation to know Him (v. 21) if the individual will only turn toward Him. Our witness is the Lord's commission to "the ends of the earth," announcing the righteousness of God available in Christ and inviting all to the personal relationship that righteousness affords. For this purpose the Spirit empowers us, that we might be His "witnesses . . . to the end of the earth" (Acts 1:8).[3]

 FAITH ALIVE

How has the Lord demonstrated to you through the years that He is the only God, the only One who molds history and redeems His people?

How do you suffer when you resist God's molding of the clay of your life? How do you benefit when you yield to Him as the Potter?

HE OUTRANKS THE GODS OF THE WORLD

Isaiah 45 ended with an appeal from the Lord for the nations of the world to bow before Him and enjoy His salvations (v. 23). Chapter 46 starts with a picture of the gods of mighty Babylon bowing in defeat and causing beasts of burden to bow beneath their weight as they cart them to "safety" from the Persian armies (vv. 1, 2).

 BEHIND THE SCENES

The Babylonian god Bel was the same as Marduk, the chief Babylonian god. He was the god of war and the patron deity of the city of Babylon. Nebo was the Babylonian god of education, literature, writing, wisdom, the arts, and sciences. The special seat of his worship was at Borsippa, near Babylon.[4] Neither Babylonian military might nor occult wisdom could protect the proud city from the Holy One of Israel and His ordained instrument Cyrus.

The gods of Babylon were being carried (Is. 46:1, 2). What did that carrying mean?

The nation of Israel was being carried (Is. 46:3, 4). What did that carrying mean?

What lesson about idolatry did Israel need to learn when they thought about idols and the Lord in terms of who carries whom? (Is. 46:5–7)

If Israel had taken the trouble to remember God's actions in the past (Is. 45:8, 9) and to listen to His message about the present, what would they have learned? (Is. 46:8–13)

 FAITH ALIVE

How do the false gods of the world that tempt us to serve them require us to work hard to "carry" them around?

Spend five minutes meditatively "listening" to the Lord and remembering all He has done for you. At the end of that time, write a brief account of how He has "carried" you and is "carrying" you.

HE CONQUERS THE WORLD

If the gods of Babylon could be carried away in humiliating defeat, Babylon herself faced a more dreadful fate. Isaiah pictured the mighty empire as an elegant lady used to finery and servants suddenly forced into slavery and shame. The Holy One of Israel who raised up Persia and tore down Babylon is the conqueror of the world.

Interpret the imagery Isaiah used to describe the humiliating of Babylon by using the following two steps:

1. Describe what was happening to the "woman" in Isaiah 47:1–3.

2. Explain how a mighty nation could be similarly brought low.

BIBLE EXTRA

Chaldeans (Is. 47:1, 5) was an ancient name for the Babylonians. In poetic passages of the Old Testament, **Chaldeans** made a handy synonym for Babylonians in parallel lines. But **Chaldeans** also connoted the practice of astrology and other occult arts (vv. 9, 12, 13). These exotic practices gave Babylon her allure as a sophisticated lady, but they also help explain why she provoked the wrath of the Holy One of Israel.

How did the Lord explain His judgment on the Babylonians?

• The first reason (Is. 47:4–7)

• The second reason (Is.47:8–11)

Of what value would the finest occult practitioners in the world be to the Babylonians when judgment came on them? (Is. 47:12, 13)

What would become of Babylon's magnificent astrologers and commercial occult artists? (Is. 47:14, 15)

Why do you think the Lord stressed His power over evil spiritual powers in Isaiah 47, the chapter that shows His ability to conquer the world?

FAITH ALIVE

People who depend on horoscopes, fortune-tellers, and other occult practices are trying to control their lives by knowledge of the future. How do you think Satan deceives and enslaves people through what they "learn" in these ways?

When Christians pay attention to occult arts—even the daily horoscope in the newspaper—what do you think happens to their dependence on God?

HE REFINES HIS PEOPLE

The nation of Judah had not been free of occultism and idolatry. The Holy One of Israel was jealous for the purity of His people and was committed to refining them of the spiritual dross that defiled them.

What spiritual advantages was Judah proud of, but what was wrong with the way she relied on them? (Is. 48:1)

How can we fall into the same trap of insincere, over-familiarity with the Lord?

How could the Israelites watch the Lord fulfill prophecy after prophecy and remain indifferent to Him? (Is. 48:3–5)

How do Christians today experience the supernatural blessings of God's Spirit and remain lukewarm to the Lord Jesus?

Why had the Lord reserved specific prophecy about the Babylonian captivity and the return from captivity under Cyrus until the ministry of Isaiah? (Is. 48:6–11)

What sudden, surprising events has the Lord used in your life to refine and purify you? How did the element of unexpectedness affect the way you responded to the Lord?

The impending refinement of Judah—historical and future—depended on the activity of three persons. What did Isaiah 48 reveal about the refining role of each?
1. The Holy One of Israel (Is. 48:12, 13)

2. The Persian emperor Cyrus (Is. 48:14, 15)

3. The Servant of the Lord (Is. 48:16)

How could the nation of Judah avoid the refining judgment of the Babylonian captivity? (Is. 48:17–19)

How can we avoid the need for the Lord to discipline us and judge the sin in our lives?

   WORD WEALTH

Teaches (Is. 48:17) translates a Hebrew verb meaning to instruct, train, or prod. The origin of the word seems to be agricultural, namely, goading cattle with a pointed stick to get them to go the right way and do the needed work. Similarly, teaching and learning are attained through a great variety of goading, by memorable events, techniques, or lessons. From this verb come the Hebrew words *talmid, melammed,* and *Talmud,* being respectively "scholar," "student," and the "Book of Rabbinic Learning."[5]

How did the Lord foresee the people of Judah responding to being refined by Him through the Babylonian captivity? (Is. 48:20, 21)

  FAITH ALIVE

Isaiah 40—66 is characterized primarily by messages of comfort (Is. 40:1, 2). Interestingly, each of the three main divisions of these chapters ends with a warning (48:22; 57:21; 66:24). How should these verses motivate the people of God who know His comfort to minister to those who need to heed these warnings?

As you examine your life right now, what are the difficulties you face that make you glad that nothing is too hard for God?

How can you depend on Him more for strength to deal with these difficulties?

1. James S. Hewett, ed., *Illustrations Unlimited* (Wheaton, IL: Tyndale House Publishers, 1988), 254.

2. *Hayford's Bible Handbook* (Nashville: Thomas Nelson, 1995), 180, "Surveying Isaiah, note on Is. 45:11."

3. Ibid., 180, "Surveying Isaiah, note on Is. 45:22, 23."

4. *Nelson's New Illustrated Bible Dictionary* (Nashville: Thomas Nelson, 1995), 509, "Gods, Pagan."

5. *Spirit-Filled Life® Bible* (Nashville, Thomas Nelson, 1991), 1025–26, "Word Wealth: Is. 48:17, teaches."

Lesson 10/The Right Man on Our Side
Isaiah 49—53

Martin Luther was so prolific a writer that one historian, when turning from Luther's work to his personal life, said, "We perceive, first of all, that he was a man, not an inkwell."[1] Luther's hymns alone are innumerable, many written just for his children. Old Lutheran hymnals were crammed with them. Modern ones still contain a good number. But almost every hymnal puts Luther's grandest hymn, "A Mighty Fortress Is Our God," in a prominent place.

Luther had a strong sense of the hostility of the devil toward humans, but a still stronger certainty that the Lord Jesus broke the power of the devil on the Cross and will defeat him every day as He protects His followers. In the second verse, Luther wrote:

> Did we in our own strength confide,
> Our striving would be losing,
> Were not the right Man on our side,
> The Man of God's own choosing.

Isaiah shared Martin Luther's passion for God's Right Man, the Stone of foundation and shelter (Is. 28:16, 17; 32:1, 2), the Light that leads to God (9:2). The Right Man is the Branch that grows from the stump to revitalize Israel after judgment (4:2; 11:1). He is the Child who will rule in justice and peace (9:6, 7). Finally He is the Suffering Servant who will bear the sins of many and redeem both Jews and Gentiles (49:6; 53:4–6).

A LIGHT TO THE GENTILES

The title Servant of the Lord first appeared as a reference to the nation of Israel (Is. 41:8–10), but quickly narrowed in focus to designate an individual embodying all of the spiritual ideals Israel never mastered (42:1–9). Amazingly, the Servant of the Lord intended to redeem Gentiles as well as Jews (42:1, 4, 6).

The first seven verses of Isaiah 49 are addressed to far-off Gentiles identified by one of Isaiah's favorite references, the "coastlands" (v. 1). Summarize the Servant's message about each of these subjects.

- His preparation to serve (Is. 49:1, 2)

- His ministry to Israel whom He represents in spiritual perfection (Is. 49:3, 4)

- His ministry to the Gentiles (Is. 49:5, 6)

- The Holy One of Israel's assessment of His Servant's future ministry (Is. 49:7)

BIBLE EXTRA

Look up these passages, and note the ways that the New Testament says Isaiah 49:5, 6 are fulfilled.
Luke 2:25–35

Acts 13:42–48

Then the Lord looked far into the future when Israel will respond in faith to Christ, the Servant of the Lord. What did He say to His Servant about these things?

- The Servant's future role in redeeming Israel (Is. 49:8, 9a)

- The future regathering of Israel (Is. 49:9b–12)

- The joy of creation when the Servant reigns in Jerusalem (Is. 49:13)

Summarize the message the Lord gave to Isaiah in response to the people of Judah who felt that He had abandoned them because of their sins (Is. 49:14).
- His love for them (Is. 49:15, 16)

- Their future deliverance (Is. 49:17, 18)

- Their future prosperity (Is. 49:19–21)

What will be the future attitude of the nations to Israel? (Is. 49:22–24)

What will be the fate of those nations that oppress the people of God? (Is. 49:24–26)

 FAITH ALIVE

How has the Lord Jesus served as a light (Is. 49:6) to show you the way to walk in the darkness of the world?

What does it mean to you to know that a mother is more likely to forget her nursing child than the Lord is to stop caring about you?

THE SERVANT WHO RESTORES ISRAEL

Although the Servant of the Lord would be a light to the Gentiles (Is. 49:6), Israel had no reason to feel neglected (v. 14). In Isaiah 50 both Lord and the Servant of the Lord assure Israel of God's abiding love as their Redeemer.

The people of Israel had compared their imagined desertion by God to two everyday calamities. What were they? (Is. 50:1a)

What was the real reason for Israel's troubles and national defeats by their enemies? (Is. 50:1b)

How did the Lord interpret Israel's lack of response to His repeated calls to national repentance and trust in Him alone? (Is. 50:2a)

How had God proven in Israel's history that He could take care of them in every difficulty? (Is. 50:2b, 3)

In the remainder of Isaiah 50, the Servant of the Lord (identified in verse 10) challenged Israel to listen to Him and accept His message. What did the Servant say about the relationship of His speaking and His listening? (Is. 50:4, 5)

In the first indication that He would suffer, what did the Servant reveal about Himself and His tormentors? (Is. 50:6)

How did the Servant explain His ability to endure suffering in terms of these topics?
- His sense of purpose (Is. 50:7)

- The presence of the Lord (Is. 50:8, 9)

- The fate of His adversaries (Is. 50:8, 9, 11)

- The company of His spiritual allies (Is. 50:10)

 FAITH ALIVE

In what kinds of circumstances are you tempted to think that God has abandoned you?

What past acts of faithfulness by the Lord remind you that He greatly loves you?

"WAKE UP!"

As Isaiah prepared to deliver the final Servant Song (Is. 52:13—53:12), the tone of his prophecy intensified. He knew that the people of Judah were not inclined to hear and believe his message (6:9, 10). He also knew that a remnant would believe (vv. 11–13), so he strengthened his appeal for repentance and faith.

What commands to pay attention repeat in these passages?

1. Isaiah 51:1, 4, 7

2. Isaiah 51:9, 17; 52:1

3. 52:11

What mood or atmosphere do these commands establish for this passage?

What did the Lord want the Israelites to learn from listening to Him about each of these?
1. Their relationship to Abraham and Sarah (Is. 51:1–3)

2. The Lord's justice and righteousness (notice the repetition of the pronouns Me, My, and I) (Is. 51:4–6)

3. The threat from Babylon (Is. 51:7, 8)

What did the Lord want Israel to awake and discover about each of these?
1. His character as Israel's Redeemer and Comforter (Is. 51:6–16)

2. The tragedy and outcome of Jerusalem's judgment (Is. 51:17–23)

3. Jerusalem's redemption from Babylonian exile (Is. 52:1–10)

How did the Lord want the exiles returning to Jerusalem to view their departure from Babylon? (Is. 52:11, 12)

FAITH ALIVE

"How beautiful upon the mountains are the feet of him who brings good news" (Is. 52:7). How would you express your gratitude for those who brought the gospel of Christ to you?

What means has the Lord used to get your attention when you have needed to wake up to some spiritual truth?

THE SERVANT: A MAN OF SORROWS

Isaiah 52:13—53:12 contains the most amazing prophecies in the Old Testament about the mission of Jesus as the Savior who died in the place of sinful humans. This final Servant Song breaks into five sections of three verses each. The first (52:13–15) and fifth (53:10–12) sections cover one subject: the final exaltation of the Servant. The second (vv. 1–3) and fourth (vv. 7–9) deal with His rejection. The heart of the song is Isaiah 53:4–6, which presents His substitutionary sacrifice for sin.

THE SUFFERING SERVANT (53:12)[2]	
Jesus understood His mission and work as the fulfillment of Isaiah's Suffering Servant.	
The Prophecy	**The Fulfillment**
He will be exalted (52:13)	Philippians 2:9
He will be disfigured by suffering (52:14; 53:2)	Mark 15:17, 19
He will make a blood atonement (52:15)	1 Peter 1:2
He will be widely rejected (53:1, 3)	John 12:37, 38
He will bear our sins and sorrows (53:4, 5)	Romans 4:25; 1 Peter 2:24, 25
He will be our substitute (53:6, 8)	2 Cornithians 5:21
He will voluntarily accept our guilt and punishment (53:7, 8)	John 10:11; 19:30
He will be buried in a rich man's tomb (53:9)	John 19:38–42
He will save us who believe in Him (53:10, 11)	John 3:16; Acts 16:31
He will die on behalf of transgressors (53:12)	Mark 15:27, 28; Luke 22:37

Before the Servant would be highly exalted (Is. 52:13), what had to happen first? (v. 14)

Who did the Lord foresee being the ones who would react in wonder to the Servant's exaltation? Why would they be astonished? (Is. 52:15)

In the first rejection passage (Is. 53:1–3), how does each of these figure in the Servant's unpopularity?
- The rejected report (Is. 53:1)

- His unimpressive appearance (Is. 53:2)

- His despised character (Is. 53:3)

At the core of this Servant Song are the verses about sin bearing. Summarize these verses.
- The punishment inherent in sin bearing (Is. 53:4)

- The healing resultant from sin bearing (Is. 53:5)

- The repentance that responds to sin bearing (Is. 53:6)

    KINGDOM EXTRA

Isaiah 53 clearly teaches that bodily healing is included in the atoning work of Christ, His suffering, and His Cross. The Hebrew words for "griefs" and "sorrows" (v. 4) specifically mean physical affliction. This is verified in the fact that

Matthew 8:17 says this Isaiah text is being exemplarily fulfilled in Jesus' healing people of human sickness and other
physical need.

The ground of provision for both our salvation and our
healing is the atoning work of Calvary. Neither is automati-
cally appropriated however; for each provision—a soul's eternal salvation or a person's temporal, physical healing—must
be received by faith. Christ's work on the Cross makes each
possible: simple faith receives each as we choose.[3]

The second rejection section (Is. 53:7–9) is more specific
than verses 1–3 because the atonement section gave Isaiah
more specifics to weave into his prophecy. How was each of
these verses fulfilled in the life and death of Jesus?

• Mute suffering (Is. 53:7)

• Execution (Is. 53:8)

• Burial (Is. 53:9)

The culminating section of the Servant Song (Is.
53:10–12) bases the exaltation of the Servant on the outcome
of His atoning sacrifice. Briefly summarize these verses.

• The grand design of the Lord (Is. 53:10)

• The finished labor of the Servant (Is. 53:11)

• The total victory of the Servant (Is. 53:12)

FAITH ALIVE

When you contemplate the suffering of Jesus on your behalf, what touches your heart most keenly?

When you think about the exalted position of Christ at the right hand of God, what do you think is the appropriate response of adoration?

When you meditate about the fact that Jesus died for your sins on the Cross, how are you moved to thank Him?

1. Will Durant, *The Reformation* (New York: Simon and Schuster, 1957), 417.

2. *Spirit-Filled Life* ® *Bible* (Nashville: Thomas Nelson, 1991), 1033, chart of The Suffering Servant.

3. Ibid., 1032, "Kingdom Dynamics: Is. 53:4, 5, Healing Prophesied Through Christ's Atonement."

Lesson 11/When Losers Will Be Winners
Isaiah 54—57

Did we in our own strength confide,
Our striving would be losing,
Were not the right Man on our side,
The Man of God's own choosing.

Martin Luther didn't always realize the power of the spiritual movement that swirled around his efforts to reform the church of the sixteenth century. He knew he led a popular movement against a privileged institution, so he wrote and spoke his most powerful messages in German rather than Latin.

As long as the educated minority of Europeans discussed their theological disagreement in Latin, 99.9% of the public didn't know and didn't care what the fuss was about. Once Luther brought the Bible and the discussion about salvation by faith alone into the German vernacular, the genie was out of the bottle and could never be imprisoned again. Peasants, craftsmen, and shopkeepers became the vanguard of the Reformation.

Men and women who had never had a stake in earlier theological debates got involved. Many educated clergy could not adjust to the idea that the opinions of unwashed peasants who lived on cabbage, turnips, and beer mattered in the least. But the Suffering Servant of Isaiah encourages the losers in the eyes of the world to believe they too can be winners with the right Man on their side.

ENLARGE THE PLACE OF YOUR TENT

For centuries, the kings of Judah had vacillated between idolatry and faithfulness to the Lord. Many of the common people had settled into a comfortable religious routine that tipped its hat to the Lord and all sorts of idols at the same time.

What hope did the Lord and His Suffering Servant offer the people of Judah who had been faithless all their lives? (Is. 54:1–3)

How did the Lord promise to treat His faithless people if they turned from their shame and disgrace to trust Him? (Is. 54:4–8)

What guarantee did the Lord offer faithless Judah that He would grant her peace and prosperity once she had learned her lessons from the judgment of the Babylonian captivity? (Is. 54:9, 10)

How did the Lord foresee the ultimate enlargement and peace of Judah and Jerusalem? (Is. 54:11–15)

What can servants of the Lord know for sure about those who oppose them? (Is. 54:16, 17)

 FAITH ALIVE

What sin that causes you shame would you like erased from your life so your relationship with God could be enlarged?

List the names of God recorded in Isaiah 54:5. What does each of these names tell you about His commitment to deal with your sin and bless you?

FAMISHED SOULS SATISFIED

Not only did the Lord and His Suffering Servant promise to enlarge the tents of repentant sinners ashamed of their sin, but They promised to satisfy the hunger and thirst of those longing for spiritual nourishment. Isaiah 55 is often considered the most overtly evangelistic chapter in the Old Testament with its appeals for faith and promises of salvation.

Using the imagery of an ancient Near Eastern food and beverage vendor, how did Isaiah present the following aspects of trusting God?

- Recognizing your need (Is. 55:1a)

- Realizing God can help (Is. 55:1b, 2b)

- Admitting the world can't help you (Is. 55:2a)

- Responding to God's promises (Is. 55:3)

"The sure mercies of David" (Is. 55:3) came through David's descendant the Messiah, the Suffering Servant of Isaiah. How will He make effective the good news that God calls hungry and thirsty sinners to Him? (Is. 55:4, 5)

What role does each of these play in the reconciliation of people to God?

- Human repentance (Is. 55:6, 7a)

- Divine response (Is. 55:7b)

Why do we need to repent—to change our way of thinking about our sins—when God never needs to change His moral attitudes? (Is. 55:8, 9)

In what ways is the Word of God like each phase of this cycle of fruitfulness? (Is. 55:10, 11)

1. Precipitation

2. Germination

3. Sprouting

4. Harvest

5. Provision

    KINGDOM EXTRA

Evangelism (the spreading of the Good News) and expansion (the enlarging of life's potential under God) both multiply by the "seed" of God's Word (Is. 55:11). Jesus described the Word as "seed" also (Luke 8:11), the source of all saving life and growth possibilities transmitted from the Father to mankind.

We never need wonder how faith is developed or how fruitfulness is realized. Faith comes by "hearing" God's Word (Rom. 10:17), that is, by receiving it wholeheartedly and humbly. Fruitfulness is the guaranteed by-product—whether for the salvation of a lost soul or the provision of a disciple's need—God's Word cannot be barren or fruitless: His own life-power is within it![1]

When God's kingdom has been established on the earth and the effects of sin removed from all creation, how will creation celebrate the goodness of God's Word and its messengers? (Is. 55:12, 13)

 ### Faith Alive

In what parts of your life and soul do you feel a hunger and thirst for God's presence and peace?

What can you do to discover and apply the parts of God's Word that could satisfy your hunger and thirst? What would you like God's Spirit to do for you through the Word?

Untouchables Will Be Saved

Isaiah 56 opens with eight verses that extend the salvation of God to repentant sinners who are social outcasts. On the one hand, these verses may seem pretty obscure; on the other hand, they offer hope to anyone who has ever felt outside the boundaries of God's love and forgiveness.

What behaviors did Isaiah associate with those who know the salvation of the Lord? (Is. 55:1, 2)

Nothing in Isaiah 55 sounded like God's free salvation could be earned by good works. In what ways can the behaviors in Isaiah 56:1 and 2 be understood as the fruits of repentance and saving faith rather than the basis of salvation?

How did the Lord regard the repentant resident alien in Judah, even though he felt despised? (Is. 56:3a, 6, 7)

How did the Lord regard the repentant eunuch whom the Law excluded from the worshiping community (Deut. 23:1)? (Is. 56:3b-5)

WORD WEALTH

Eunuch (Is. 56:4) translates a Hebrew word with an ordinary and a technical meaning. The ordinary, literal meaning referred to a castrated man. The technical meaning referred to a court official. Probably many officials originally had been castrated to eliminate their threat to establish a rival dynasty or to make them safe around the wives of kings and emperors. During biblical times, most officials called "eunuchs" were physically intact.

Israel did not castrate men, or even animals (Lev. 22:24). A childless man was as unthinkable as a childless woman. Accordingly, an impotent man was excluded from the worshiping community of Israel (Deut. 23:1). Isaiah's message of hope to eunuchs meant God's salvation through the Suffering Servant excluded no one.

How broadly did the Lord commit Himself to touching the untouchables with His grace? (Is. 56:8)

FAITH ALIVE

Who are the people in your community who are generally despised or avoided?

How could you or your church become involved in sharing the love of Christ with these groups or individuals?

PSYCHOLOGY OF IDOLATRY

Isaiah wrote a great deal about idols and idolatry in chapters 40—66. Usually the prophet stressed the lifelessness of the idols and the folly of the idolaters. In 56:9—57:13, Isaiah turned a more analytical eye toward his countrymen who pursued false gods and assessed why they turned their lives down these spiritual dead-end streets.

When Isaiah looked at the religious and political leaders of Judah who weren't following the Lord, what did he find motivating their careless leadership? (Is. 56:9–12)

What do you think is wrong with a society and its values when no one cares when its righteous and merciful citizens die and don't even know that they have gone to be with the Lord? (Is. 57:1, 2)

Isaiah addressed his countrymen who practiced a fertility religion that combined occultism and ritual immorality (Is. 57:3). How did the prophet describe the attitudes of these idolators toward each of these?

- Righteous people (Is. 57:4)

- Their children (Is. 57:5b)

- Their worship (Is. 57:5, 6)

- Sexual excesses (Is. 57:7–9)

- Their hope (Is. 57:10)

Why had the idolators felt they could get away with ignoring the Lord and pursuing their selfish, carnal ways? (Is. 57:11)

What was wrong with their reasoning that they could worship any god they wanted to? (Is. 57:11–13)

 FAITH ALIVE

What kinds of people in the world around you reflect the attitudes Isaiah attributed to the idolators of his day?

What aspects of biblical truth do they need to hear to warn them of the fate that awaits them if they do not repent and turn to the Lord for salvation?

BACKSLIDERS CAN BE SAVED

Isaiah did not end his discussion about the idolatry of his countrymen without including an appeal for the backslider to repent and return to the Lord. This was the last kind of "loser" Isaiah encouraged to become a winner by repenting and enjoying the blessings of God.

Once again Isaiah employed his imagery of preparing a road in the wilderness so people can return to the Lord (Is. 57:14; see 40:3-5). How do you think the way needed to be prepared for Judah's idolatrous backsliders?

Describe God and the kind of person He wants to dwell with Him. Why do you think this great contrast is necessary? (Is. 57:15)

Why does the Lord use both the "stick" of judgment and the "carrot" of mercy in recovering a backsliding believer? What does He accomplish with each? (Is. 57:16–18)

Contrast the fates of backsliders who respond to the judgment and mercy of God and those who do not. (Is. 57:19, 21)

     FAITH ALIVE

When have you felt your life was like the wicked man's in Isaiah 57:20, churning up mire and dirt?

How has the Lord worked in your experiences to bring peace and wholeness to these areas of agitation and confusion?

1. *Spirit-Filled Life® Study Bible* (Nashville: Thomas Nelson, 1991), 1036, "Kingdom Dynamics: Is. 55:10, 11, God's Word, Evangelism, and Expansion."

Lesson 12/Our God Reigns
Isaiah 58—61

The lion was proud of his mastery of the animal realm, so one day he decided to tour the jungle to check on the obedience of his subjects. He went straight to the rhinoceros. "Who is the king of the jungle?" the lion growled.

"Why you are of course," the rhinoceros stammered.

The lion gave a mighty roar of approval.

Next he asked the tiger, "Who is the king of the jungle?"

The tiger bowed and answered quickly, "O mighty lion, everyone knows it's you."

Next the lion found an aged elephant who happened to suffer from a painful tusk. "Who is the king of the jungle?" the lion asked with an earth-shaking roar that made the elephant's tusk throb and her head pound.

The old elephant seized the lion in her trunk, whirled him overhead, and slammed him against a tree, pounded him on the ground by his tail, and dunked him in the watering hole until he stopped making bubbles. Finally she tossed the half-dead lion on the bank and sauntered off.

The lion staggered to his feet, coughed up half the watering hole, and looked around at the crowd of hyenas and monkeys that had gathered to watch. "Just because she didn't know the answer, she didn't need to get mean about it," he said haughtily and limped into the underbrush.

Through the prophet Isaiah, the Lord made certain that no one could think that the Holy One of Israel was such a king as this unfortunate lion. Only the living God could make the heavens and the earth, foretell the future, and control the destinies of nations and individual men and women. Only He reigns in heaven above and on earth below.

To Stamp Out Self-Righteousness

Isaiah turned from condemning the idolatry Israel and Judah had struggled with so long to anticipate the dead ritualism that would vie with true belief after the Babylonian captivity would be over. With a voice like a trumpet, Isaiah exposed the newest deadly sin of God's people (Is. 58:1). How would they behave and what appearance would they give? (Is. 58:2)

What was wrong with the fancy fasts that the prophet foresaw God's people engaging in as proof of their spirituality?
- Their complaint (Is. 58:3a)

- Their hidden behavior (Is. 58:3b, 4)

- Their public behavior (Is. 58:5)

Look up these verses and describe the kind of fast the Lord approves of for His people.
- (Is. 58:6, 7) Behaviors accompanying a proper fast

- (Is. 58:8, 9a) Results from a proper fast

 Kingdom Extra

The power of the fast is directly related to God's involvement. We certainly can decide to fast as we wish; however, the result may be that we simply go without food. When we respond to the "call of the Lord to fast" there is no telling what He has in mind to accomplish! Scripture teaches us that the power of the fast breaks bondage in individuals and weakens the oppression of the enemy. We can be certain that if we respond obediently He will accomplish great and mighty things as a result of our partnering with Him in His fast.[1]

How did the Lord describe the spiritual renewal that the returned exiles from Babylon would regularly need?

- Their ongoing, self-righteous sins (Is. 58:9b, 10a)

- The Lord's promises to them (Is. 58:10b, 11)

- The glory awaiting them (Is. 59:12)

The returning exiles also would turn Sabbath observance into a legalistic nightmare whose observance fed self-righteous vanities more than led to genuine worship of the Holy One of Israel (Is. 58:13, 14). How do you think a person can devote a day to worship so that it is a spiritual delight rather than a self-righteous chore?

 FAITH ALIVE

Fasting and Sabbath observance aren't the practices that tempt us to show off our self-righteousness today. What do you think are the practices or behaviors that tempt us to try to appear righteous?

Self-righteous practices usually are distortions of true righteousness, such as fasting and Sabbath observance. How do the practices you listed in the previous question relate to issues of true righteousness?

TO REDEEM THE REPENTANT

During the lifetime of Isaiah, the citizens of Judah needed to repent of their idolatry if the Lord was to reign over them. During the Babylonian captivity, the exiles would need to repent of their doubts that God was still in control. After the Jews returned to Judah, they would need to repent of spiritual indifference and formal religion without faith.

Isaiah reported that the people of God felt separated from Him. Why was this?

- The impossible reason (Is. 59:1)

- The real reason (Is. 59:2)

As Isaiah contemplated the sins of God's people, how did he see each of these parts of their lives involved?

- Their hands (Is. 59:3a)

- Their speech (Is. 59:3b, 4)

- Their plans (Is. 59:5, 6)

- Their path of life (Is. 59:7, 8)

Explain how each of these pictures are part of what it's like living with unconfessed sin.

- Groping for the wall in the dark (Is. 59:9, 10)

- Growling like bears and moaning like doves (Is. 59:11)

- Living with a nagging conscience (Is. 59:12)

- Truth lies dead in the street, while justice and righteousness have been run out of town (Is. 59:14)

Why did the Lord finally have to act personally in the history of His people? (Is. 59:15b, 16a)

How did the Lord picture Himself bringing judgment on Judah and the surrounding nations? (Is. 59:16–18)

How did the Lord describe His salvation for the repentant?

• The protection His reign provides (Is. 59:19)

• The ones whom He protects (Is. 59:20)

• The covenant He makes with the repentant (Is. 59:21)

 KINGDOM EXTRA

"My Spirit . . . is upon you, and My words . . . shall not depart from your mouth" (Is. 59:21). Spiritual victory is assured as the Lord marches fully armed against His enemies (vv. 17, 18), offering redemptive relationship to those accepting His victory (v. 20). Even when the enemy's resistance carries the force of mighty waters, the Spirit raises the battle standard—Christ's victory on the Cross—rallying the righteous sons of Zion (v. 19), those who will stand with Messiah to rule with Him. Through the new covenant we can have God's empowering Spirit upon us, equipping us for spiritual warfare (Eph. 6:10–18)—and the charismatic word gifts become a continuous flow of prophetic victory proclamation (1 Cor. 12:7–11).[2]

FAITH ALIVE

When the Lord has prompted you to confess and repent of sins in your life, how have you experienced the blessings of Isaiah 59:21?
  1. God's Spirit upon you

  2. God's words in your mouth

TO ESTABLISH HIS CAPITAL

As you near the end of the book of Isaiah, you will find that God's Spirit prompted the prophet to write more and more about the new heavens and new earth and the new Jerusalem at the end of time. Isaiah 60 describes the restored Holy City. Our God reigns, and this will be His capital city.

Isaiah announced that in the future Jerusalem would be prominent and brightly glorious (Is. 60:1). How will Jerusalem's future glory relate to each of these?

• The glory of God (Is. 60:1b, 2b)

• The darkness of the nations (Is. 60:2)

• The position of God relative to Jerusalem (Is. 60:2b, 19, 20)

• The response of gentile believers (Is. 60:3)

Describe the future blessing of Jerusalem in each of these categories.

• The return of the scattered (Is. 60:4, 8, 9)

- Wealth (Is. 60:5–7)

- Security (Is. 60:10–12)

- Center of worship (Is. 60:13–16)

- Plenty and excellence (Is. 60:17, 18)

In what three ways did Isaiah summarize the future glory of Jerusalem as the capital of the divine King?
1. Isaiah 60:19, 20

2. Isaiah 60:21

3. Isaiah 60:22

 FAITH ALIVE

Read Revelation 21:22–27 and 22:5. What points of contact do you see between these passages and Isaiah 60?

What encouragement do you derive from the prospect of sharing the New Jerusalem with the Father, the Son, and all of God's people?

TO BLESS HIS SUBJECTS

Isaiah 61 begins with the words of the Suffering Servant promising the salvation of God and ends with the words of

God's people rejoicing in that salvation. Our God reigns supremely when He is glorified in the lives of redeemed men and women who bear His image in righteousness and holiness.

What roles did the Holy Spirit and God the Father play in the ministry of God the Son as the Suffering Servant? (Is. 61:1)

List the seven infinitive phrases in Isaiah 61:1–3 that summarize the ministry of the Messiah.

1.

2.

3.

4.

5.

6.

7.

 BIBLE EXTRA

Compare Isaiah 61:1, 2 with Luke 4:16–21, and note which parts Jesus quotes and which He leaves out. How did Jesus understand this part of Isaiah to be fulfilled?

Read the rest of Luke 4, through verse 43. Now read
this excerpt from *Hayford's Bible Handbook* that explains how
the saving reign of God—the kingdom of God—has arrived in
the earthly ministry of Jesus and will be completed with the
Second Coming of Christ.

All that Jesus did is related to this claim that the
kingdom of God has dawned through His ministry. His
healings were manifestations of the presence of the
kingdom. In these deeds there was direct confrontation
between God and the forces of evil. . . . Summarizing
His ministry, Jesus declared, "I saw Satan fall like light-
ning from heaven" (Luke 10:18). Satan and evil are in
retreat now that the kingdom has made its entrance into
human history. . . . (1 John 2:17). . . .

Although the Gospels . . . focus on the present
aspect of the kingdom . . . , it . . . will be realized per-
fectly only at the Second Coming. The kingdom that
comes through the ministry of Jesus dawns in the form
of a mystery. Although it is physically present in the
deeds and words of Jesus, it does not overwhelm the
world. The judgment of God's enemies is postponed.
The kingdom that arrived with Jesus did not include the
triumphal entry so longed for by the Jews. It arrived
secretly like leaven, or like a small pearl of great value
that can be hidden in one's pocket (Matt. 13:31–46).[3]

The Lord promises to bless His people so they will be like
"trees of righteousness" that He has planted to His glory (Is.
61:3c). Describe what each of these passages adds to the
description of these rooted, fruitful people of God in:

• Isaiah 61:4

• Isaiah 61:5

• Isaiah 61:6

- Isaiah 61:7, 8

- Isaiah 61:9

How does Isaiah use these images to express the joy of the people of God because of God's blessing?
- Fine clothing (Is. 61:10)

- A garden in the spring (Is. 61:11)

 FAITH ALIVE

In what ways has the Lord blessed you with "beauty for ashes" (Is. 61:3) through your saving relationship with Jesus Christ?

How have you found that the "garment of praise" can protect your heart from "the spirit of heaviness" (Is. 61:3)?

1. *Hayford's Bible Handbook* (Nashville: Thomas Nelson, 1995), 182, "Surveying Isaiah, note on Is. 58:6."
2. Ibid., 182–183, "Surveying Isaiah, note on Is. 59:21.
3. Ibid., 667.

Lesson 13/Marching to Zion
Isaiah 62—66

After the first four Crusades had failed to free the Holy Land, a twelve-year-old shepherd boy named Stephen amassed 20,000 children in France to march to Zion. They hiked to Marseilles where the waters of the Mediterranean were supposed to open before them. When the ocean stayed put, "generous" shipowners packed them on seven cargo vessels and sent them on their way—to slavery in North Africa. Frederick II, the Holy Roman Emperor, hanged the shipowners.[1]

Telling God it's time to launch the last days has always been a foolish—occasionally deadly—activity. The Lord Himself said of the New Jerusalem, "I, the Lord, will hasten it in its time" (Is. 60:22). But there is a sense in which we are marching to Zion every day spiritually. How we "march" through life determines our preparation for the future literal event.

> We're marching to Zion,
> Beautiful, beautiful Zion.
> We're marching upward to Zion,
> The Beautiful city of God.

THE GOAL OF THE PILGRIMS

The presence of God is represented for all of the people of God—believing Jews and Gentiles—by the vision of the New Jerusalem. In the final chapters of Isaiah the attention of the prophet and of the Lord is fixed more and more on the Holy City as it will be when the Lord reigns on earth.

What will Jerusalem one day mean to the following?

- The Gentiles (Is. 62:1, 2a)

- The Lord (Is. 62:2b–4)

- The descendants of Israel (Is. 62:5)

What role did Isaiah envision prophets and other spiritual "watchmen" playing in God's blessing of Jerusalem? (Is. 62:6, 7)

What is the Lord's promise for Jerusalem?

- Concerning prosperity (Is. 62:8, 9)

- Concerning salvation of His people (Is. 62:10, 11)

- Concerning the fame of His City (Is. 62:12)

 KINGDOM EXTRA

Isaiah foresaw the coming of Christ a second time and identified those who are with Him. The identification of the sought-out city (Is. 62:11) is none other than the church of Jesus, the New Jerusalem (Heb. 12:22). In his revelation of Jesus, John also identifies the New Jerusalem as the church in Revelation 3:12, and specifically as coming down from heaven (Rev. 21:2, 10). In this light, the living church has reason for a joy-filled existence and a Spirit-filled impetus for mission.[2]

FAITH ALIVE

What does it do to your sense of self-worth to know that you are a member of the sought-out people of God?

How should you approach the responsibilities and difficulties of your life differently as someone God has sought out and will not forsake?

THE JUDGE OF THE SINNERS

In Isaiah 61:2 the Servant of the Lord said He was "To proclaim the acceptable year of the Lord, and the day of vengeance of our God." Chapter 62 expanded on "the acceptable year of the Lord" and chapter 63 opens with six verses describing "the day of vengeance of our God." "The acceptable year of our Lord" and "the day of vengeance of our God" are two sides of the same coin, different aspects of the two comings of Christ.

What did the watchman on Jerusalem's wall (Is. 62:6) see approaching from the south? (Is. 63:1)

How did the Stranger answer the watchman? (Is. 63:1c)

What did the watchman want to know about the Stranger? (Is. 63:2)

How did the Stranger explain His gory garments? (Is. 63:3–6)

BIBLE EXTRA

Isaiah 63:1–6 has no Old Testament parallel. It depicts Yahweh in bloodstained garments returning from annihilating the enemies of His people. Edom (v. 1) was a territory southeast of the Dead Sea, inhabited by the descendants of Esau; the name Edom means "Red." That nation was usually in conflict with Judah, and Edom became a symbol for wicked nations.[3]

Read Revelation 14:14–20 and 19:11–16. What parts of John's revelation depend on the earlier revelation in Isaiah 63?

What is new in Revelation that enlarges on God's earlier message through Isaiah?

 FAITH ALIVE

Obviously the proper response to the future destruction of the wicked is *not* to gloat that they will be squashed like grapes. How do you think Christians should respond to each of these aspects of God's ultimate judgment of the wicked?

• The justice of judgment

• The wrath of God directed at sin

• The suffering of sinners who are judged

THE PRAYER OF THE SPIRIT-FILLED PILGRIMS

Isaiah 63:7—64:12 consists of a beautiful prayer that the prophet offered the Lord on behalf of all His people who remember His mighty deeds in the past and trust Him to care for them now and forever more. Isaiah projected himself into the future and joined the likes of Jeremiah, Daniel, Ezra, and Nehemiah in confessing the corporate sins of Israel and asking the Lord to restore His people after purifying them of sins by means of the chastening of the Babylonian captivity.

Describe these bases of Isaiah's prayer.

- The Lord's love for His people (Is. 63:7, 8)

- The Lord's redemption of His people (Is. 63:9)

- The Lord's chastening of His people (Is. 63:10)

Why do you think it is the Holy Spirit rather than the Father or Son who experiences grief when the people of God sin? (Is. 63:10; see Eph. 4:30)

As Isaiah prepared to intercede for Israel in his lifetime, he looked back at God's activity at the time of the Exodus from Egypt (Is. 63:11-14). What did the prophet remember about the Lord's past deliverance that he wanted repeated after the Babylonian captivity?

In your Bible underline all of the imperative verbs the prophet addressed to God in Isaiah 63:15—64:12. Then circle the various names for God that the prophet used in this petitionary part of his prayer. (God is addressed as "Father" only in this prayer in the book of Isaiah.)

What kinds of things do you think Isaiah hoped to accomplish by asking God to "come down" and to "return"?

What significance does each name for God have for this prayer?

FAITH ALIVE

What do you learn from Isaiah 63:15—64:12 about the offensiveness of your sins against God?

How could you improve the way you confess your sins on the basis of Isaiah's prayer?

THE NEW JERUSALEM FOR GOD'S ELECT

Isaiah prayed on behalf of the people of Israel, but he knew that most people in Judah and Jerusalem did not share his spirit of repentance. When the Lord speaks in Isaiah 65 right after the prophet ends his prayer, He makes it clear that the New Jerusalem is for the righteous remnant from Israel and the nations of the earth.

How did Isaiah describe each of these?

* Believing Gentiles (Is. 65:1)

* Rebellious Israel (Is. 65:2–4)

* The Lord (Is. 65:5)

What good things did the Lord have to say about the believing remnant of Israel? (Is. 65:8–10)

What bad things did He have to say about the rebellious majority of Israel? (Is. 65:11, 12)

How did the Lord contrast the believing remnant with the rebellious majority of Israel? (Is. 65:13–16)

Remnant	Rebels

What are the two new creations of God at the end of time for His elect remnant? What will be their outcomes?

Creation I (Is. 65:17)	Creation II (Is. 65:18, 19)
Outcome I	Outcome II

How did the Lord describe life in the New Jerusalem of the new heavens and earth? (Is. 65:20–25)

FAITH ALIVE

Read Revelation 21:1–8. How is the vision of John like the vision of Isaiah?

How does the sense of rejoicing associated with the New Jerusalem (Is. 65:18, 19; Rev. 2—4) motivate you to serve the Lord and eagerly expect His Second Coming?

TRUE WORSHIP IN THE NEW JERUSALEM

Like the book of Revelation, the prophecies of Isaiah end with a description of the kind of worship that will characterize the New Jerusalem. Unlike Revelation, the book of Isaiah continues to contrast the blessedness of the worshipers in Jerusalem with the misery of those who are objects of the wrath of God.

How did the Lord reach the following conclusion about worship?

1. A temple is unnecessary (Is. 66:1, 2a)

2. A humble heart is necessary (Is. 66:2b)

How does God react to these false forms of worship?

• Meaningless ritual? (Is. 66:3, 4)

• Religious persecution (Is. 66:5, 6)

Describe these aspects of the future of the New Jerusalem as a worshiping community.
- The speed of its establishment (Is. 66:7–9)

- The joy of its glory (Is. 66:10, 11)

- The comfort of its peace (Is. 66:12, 13)

What difference does it make whether a person experiences "the hand of the Lord" or "His indignation" when the Lord appears to "judge all flesh"? (Is. 66:14–17)

How will believing Jews and Gentiles cooperate in the New Jerusalem to glorify the Lord? (Is. 66:18–21)

What are the eternal destinies awaiting believers and unbelievers? (Is. 66:22–24)

 KINGDOM EXTRA

Spirit-filled believers should understand that the Father desires to burn away anything of flesh in us today (Is. 66:15,

16). The presence of the Holy Spirit (in the familiar form of fire) and the Word (in the familiar form of a sword) assures us that God's Word under the touch of His Spirit will be all that is required to ready His church for that concluding moment.[4]

How is the fire of God's Spirit and the sword of His Word cleansing your life now in preparation for eternity with Him?

What are your greatest motivations for welcoming the cleansing work of God's Spirit and Word in your daily life?

THE HOLY ONE OF ISRAEL SAVES—ISAIAH 40—66

In lesson 1 you were asked to look up a series of verses to locate dominant ideas in Isaiah. They were 1) the Holy One of Israel, 2) salvation, and 3) the Servant of the Lord. Combine the three, and you have a good summary of the book—especially Isaiah 40—66: The Holy One of Israel saves through His Suffering Servant.

Look up these groups of passages and write final summaries of major ideas in Isaiah 40—66.

• Isaiah 40:1–3; 51:1–3; 61:2, 3; 66:12, 13

• Isaiah 40:18–20; 44:9–20; 46:1, 2, 6, 7

• Isaiah 42:1–4; 49:1–6; 50:4–9; 52:13—53:12

• Isaiah 40:9; 46:12, 13; 51:3, 11; 52:1–3, 7–9; 60:13–22; 62:1–12

Based on this review of Isaiah 40—66, describe as specifically as you can
• The ways in which God's saving reign is already present in the world.

• The ways in which God's saving reign is still to come.

How does your growing understanding of God's present and future saving reign affect your prayers for the Second Coming of Christ?

1. Will Durant, *The Age of Faith* (New York: Simon and Schuster, 1950), 606.

2. *Hayford's Bible Handbook* (Nashville: Thomas Nelson, 1995), 183, "Surveying Isaiah, note on Is. 62:11, 12."

3. *Spirit-Filled Life® Bible* (Nashville: Thomas Nelson, 1991), 1045, notes on Is. 63:1–6 and 63:1.

4. *Hayford's Bible Handbook,* 183–184, "Surveying Isaiah, note on Is. 66:15, 16."

SPIRIT-FILLED LIFE® BIBLE DISCOVERY GUIDE SERIES

*Coming Soon

SPIRIT-FILLED LIFE® KINGDOM DYNAMICS STUDY GUIDES

OTHER SPIRIT-FILLED LIFE® STUDY RESOURCES